# Performative Revolution in Egypt:

## An Essay in Cultural Power

JEFFREY C. ALEXANDER

BLOOMSBURY ACADEMIC

First published in 2011 by
Bloomsbury Academic
an imprint of Bloomsbury Publishing Plc
36 Soho Square, London W1D 3QY, UK
and
175 Fifth Avenue, New York, NY 10010, USA
Copyright © Jeffrey C. Alexander 2011.

CIP records for this book are available from the
British Library and the Library of Congress
ISBN 978-1-78093-045-9 (paperback)
ISBN 978-1-78093-088-6 (ebook)

This book is produced using paper that is made from wood grown
in managed, sustainable forests. It is natural, renewable and
recyclable. The logging and manufacturing processes
conform to the environmental regulations of
the country of origin.

Printed and bound in Great Britain by
the MPG Books Group, Bodmin, Cornwall

Cover image: ©Yannis Behrakis/Reuters

**www.bloomsburyacademic.com**

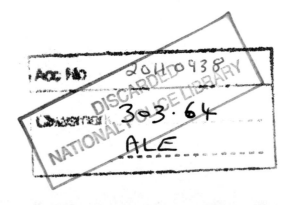

# Performative Revolution in Egypt

*For Roger Friedland*

# Contents

# Preface

N 1971, when Henry Kissinger asked Zhou Enlai his opinion of the French Revolution, the Chinese premier is said to have famously replied it was too early to tell. It certainly is also too early to understand the effects of the revolution that took place in Egypt earlier this year. Yet, regardless of how the "25 January Revolution" will eventually be judged, the eighteen-day upheaval that overthrew not only a dictator but his massive supporting regime was a world-historical event. With Tunisia as background and trigger, it constitutes the most important democratic movement in the history of the Arab world. Future journalists, historians, and social scientists will spill an ocean of ink unpacking its historical ramifications and parsing its causes. Many will argue that "25 January" was not, in fact, a revolution at all, for economic interests were not immediately changed and because it was mostly just a political realignment after all. They will be wrong.

This essay is devoted less to the "why" of the Egyptian revolution than the "how". But the how is crucial for understanding the why. How it happened explains why there was a revolution in Egypt in the year 2011, from 25 January to 11 February.

In its Arabic television reporting on the tense and violent clashes of 28 January, an Al Jazeera journalist spoke about "the consciousness that is reflected in the streets."[1] It is consciousness – internal, subjective, and collective – that makes revolutionary movements move. To understand the making of a revolution we must look at it from within, from the inside. What did it mean to those who participated in it, and how did they project these internal meanings to the outside? The Egyptian revolution was a living drama whose political success depended on its cultural power: its ability to project powerful symbols and real-time performances, plot-compelling protagonists and despicable antagonists; to stimulate and circulate powerful emotions; to organize exemplary solidarity; to create suspense; and finally to minister ignominious defeat to dark and polluted adversaries while purifying the nation through a stunning victory that lifted citizens to new hope and glory.

To gain access to dramatic meaning, we must examine collective representations. We can understand how social actors feel and think and imagine only by looking at how they symbolically represent their social experience. These symbolic representations are collective, not in the sense that everybody shares them exactly but by virtue of their being public not private, contributing to an emergent language that allows actors to communicate new experiences as they unfold. As movement actors represent new experiences to themselves, they project these understandings to others, to participants and to those watching on the sidelines from near and far. These collective representations are filtered by the mass media and projected back to participants and audiences in turn.

Social scientists and journalists want their analyses to be

realistic, yet an historical event can never be confronted as such, as a pristine and neutral social fact separated from the relativism of subjective understanding. When we examine an event, we encounter not the thing in itself but representations of what happened – by those on the scene, by outsiders interpreting it, by those who challenge emerging meanings with others. To understand the accumulating, splitting, narrating, upsurging, declining, polluting, and purifying representations that drove the Egyptian revolution is to understand the reality that made it. To assert that something hidden beneath representations is what really caused the revolution – a more "really real" material or demographic reality – is just that, an assertion. Theoretical conjectures about an invisible but truly determinative cause – a hard structural base underneath slippery symbols – seem plausible only if subjective references to such a putative reality can be found among actors' representations. In which case, the material elements said to be buried underneath social action become only putative, so-called causes. Without being mediated by cultural representations material causes would not have effect.

The principal data for the following exercise in cultural sociology are collective representations circulated by mass media. Mass media provide not only factual information about what happened and when, but thousands of direct quotes from participants in the revolution; they also report observations and interpretations by journalists so deeply immersed in the Egyptian scene that they might be called lay ethnographers – in spite of themselves. True, journalists were not neutral observers of the events that unfolded in Egypt; most were deeply committed, not only personally but institutionally, to the same ideals of democracy and civil society as those espoused by the revolutionaries themselves. In their exercise of interpretive judgment, however, these lay ethnographers were detached and impersonal. Disciplined by professional ethics, journalists evaluated whether or not the actions and words of the regime's supporters and antagonists corresponded with the reporters' own value commitments, and they described and commented upon these representations accordingly.

The data for this interpretive essay are drawn primarily from reports filed in Cairo by journalists for media institutionally based in the United States, United Kingdom, France, Italy, and Qatar, from 23 January to 21 February 2011, but concentrating on the eighteen-day period from 25 January to 11 February. I have also sampled the Facebook page, 'We Are All Khaled Said', a post maintained by leaders of the revolutionary movement, in both its English and Arabic forms; television coverage of the ongoing events by Al Jazeera in English and Arabic; and articles and commentaries on the Al Jazeera (Arabic) website. I have also examined the speeches and official statements of American and Egyptian public officials via both independent and government websites.

The most thorough sampling was from the *New York Times*, where I looked at 484 separate news reports, editorials, and columns, and selected 266 of these for concentrated analysis. While left-leaning in its editorial policies, the *New York Times* remains the newspaper of record in the United States. Its reportorial and editing resources are significantly larger than any other American news medium, its website is by far the most frequently visited, and its coverage largely sets the agenda for national and international reporting, not only for other American print media but for the nation's television and radio news reporting. The *New York Times'* news coverage overlaps to a high degree with that of the *Wall Street Journal*, despite the latter's editorial pages being decidedly to the right. This overlap is the product, not only of the *Times'* influence, but of the widespread professionalization of the journalistic field in the United States. I have extensively examined the *Journal*'s coverage of the Egyptian events, as well as that of *USA Today*, a more "popular" and less sophisticated, more tabloid-style daily newspaper that has the highest daily circulation in the United States. Outside the United States, I examined coverage in the *Guardian* in the United Kingdom, *Le Monde* in France, *La Repubblica* in Italy, and Al Jazeera, in English and Arabic, the Qatar-based news service that has become the major news and interpretive resource inside the Arab world for independent information about current events.

Among these news sources, accounts of the Egyptian revolution – of its key events and actors, their motives and their relations – differed in no significant respect, at least concerning the issues I address here. This remarkable media convergence generates confidence that the empirical "data" of this essay are reliable. The myriad events reported here did happen; people and groups did react in the ways I describe; they did offer the justifications and attributions to which I refer. While the interpretations I offer for these events, actions, and justifications are my own, the manuscript has been read by native Arab-speakers who participated in the revolutionary events, and I have had access to raw ethnographic field notes recording their impressions during those days. The text includes extensive notes to provide background information as well as sources, but readers will be able to trace the unfurling of events without constant reference to them.

I am indebted to Mira Debs for her invaluable research and reflections, and I thank the following students and colleagues for feedback on earlier versions of this essay: John Hartley, Farhad Khosrokhavar, Jonathan Wyrtzen, Andreas Hess, Erik Ringmar, Giuseppe Sciortino, Atef Said, Werner Binder, Elizabeth Breese, Ron Eyerman, Eric Woods, Kate Nash, Luke Wagner, Vered Vinitsky-Seroussi, and Soha Al Saman. Caroline Wintersgill, of Bloomsbury Academic, provided helpful editorial suggestions and Nadya Jaworsky and Nadine Amalfi critical editorial support. I am grateful to Omar Mumallah for his guidance through the Arabic media and for his translations.

"Sometimes you know the story. Sometimes you make it up as you go along and have no idea how it will come out. Everything changes as it moves. That is what makes the movements which make the story."

Ernest Hemingway

"Performance always exceeds its space and its image, since it lives only in its own doing."

Jill Dolan

DISCUSSIONS about revolutions, from the social scientific to the journalistic, almost invariably occur in the realist mode. Whether nominalist or collectivist, materialist, political or institutional, it seems a point of honor to maintain that it is real issues, real groups, and real interests, and how these have affected relative power vis-à-vis the state, that determine who makes revolutions, who opposes them, and who wins at the end of the day.

At the very beginning of the "25 January Revolution" in Egypt, a reporter for the *New York Times* traced its temporal and spatial origins to the naturalistic causal power of a single event: "The beating of a young businessman named Khaled Said last year [in Alexandria] led to weeks of demonstrations against police brutality."[2] Said, a twenty-eight-year-old businessman, allegedly had filmed proof of police corruption; he was dragged from an internet café on 6 June 2010, tortured, and beaten to death. Addressing the broader social origins of the revolution, the *New York Times* also ran the headline, "Jobs and Age Reign as Factors in Mideast Uprisings," with an op-ed columnist explaining that "these are solid measures, but I would add spending on essentials like food" and "income inequality and burgeoning Internet usage" as other factors.[3] A *Le Monde* journalist noted that, while the revolutionary slogans were primarily political, "recent price increases and rising unemployment have become powerful engines of Egyptian protest."[4] A *Guardian* reporter also situated the protests in material concerns, "a wave of protest, sparked by self-immolation, unemployment and high food prices, sweeps the Arab world from Mauritania to Saudi Arabia."[5] The BBC webpage "Twenty Reasons Why It's Kicking Off Everywhere" cited "economic failure" and the "demographic bulge," adding that "at the heart of it all is a new sociological type: the graduate with no future;" that "women [are] very numerous as the backbone;" that "people just know more than they used to" and "have a better understanding of power;" that "truth moves faster than lies;" that "technology has expanded;" and that "the network [is] more powerful than the hierarchy."[6]

Western news media were quick to assure readers that the Egyptian revolution was not "ideological" or "moralistic,"[7] that its demands were down to earth and "concrete."[8] There was a collapse of living conditions, suffering groups rebelled, demography mattered, and the sharing of information was crucial. Eventually, state repression faltered. As for what happened next, it was a matter for the stronger to decide. Posing the question, "who is really controlling events," a *New York Times* essayist supplied the conventional wisdom: "Lenin understood that the ultimate question in each revolution is always the unfathomable alchemy of power: who controls whom." Lenin himself put it more succinctly: "Who whom?"[9] Academic explanations of revolutions differ in detail and sophistication, but not in kind. An influential French demographer linked the "Arab Spring" to falling birth rates and rising rates of literacy, citing these as sure indicators of modern democratic "*mentalités*."[10]

This essay takes a different approach. I will not argue that such so-called social factors are without significance, but that, in themselves, social facts do not speak. It is representations of social facts that do the talking. When wages and unemployment, birth rates and literacy, youth, the new class and the old state, corruption, repression, and urban decay enter into the tumultuous back and forth of revolutionary social strife, they do so as signs, folding these empirical facts ("signifieds" in semiotic terms) into chains of already powerful symbols ("signifiers"). But, while their materiality is an illusion, their factuality is not: it is a useful fiction. It is the apparent naturalness of signified social facts that gives symbolic constructions their extraordinary pragmatic and performative effect. Social facts enter into history as meanings, not only to outsiders but to revolutionaries themselves.[11]

At the core of social meanings are binary codes that categorize things in moral terms, as good and bad, as pure-sacred and as polluted-profane. When these deeply felt moral-cum-expressive evaluations are wrapped in the clothing of human protagonists and antagonists, they structure the dynamic social narratives marking revolutionary time. These stories establish the execrable origins of social suffering, the past from which contemporary revolutionary struggle has developed, and the endpoint of justice and social transformation, the future to which struggles in the present are plotted to proceed.[12]

*Figure 1*   'We Are All Khaled Said' Facebook Page[13]

**'We Are All Khaled Said' — English Translation**

Administrator (Wael Ghonim) January 27, 5:49 a.m.)

حاسس إني باحلم"

"Feeling that I'm Dreaming."

Eyad Irshaid (Jan. 27, 5:50a.m.)

هناك جديد؟

"Something new?"

Mohammed Abo El-ella (Jan. 27, 5:50 a.m.)

حقيقه IIIIIIIIIIIIIIIIIIII لاا [sic] مش حلم.

"Noooooooooooo, [It is] reality, not dream!"

Mido Sheba (Jan. 27 @ 5:50 a.m.)

احلم الحلم بقي حقيقة

"I dream the dream comes true."

Taghreed Ahmed (Jan 27, 7:50 a.m.)

والله واحنا كلنا حاسين اننا في حلم

"By God, we all are feeling that we are in a dream."

Bannour Grodt (Jan 27, 5:50 a.m.)

كيف ستحس اذن هروب مبارك الى السعودية؟

"[And] How will you feel when Mubarak runs to Saudi [Arabia]?"

Esraa Hyman (Jan. 27, 5:50 a.m.)

و باذن الله خير... حاسة اني في حرب بس النصر
لينا باذن الله

"It feels like I am in a war but victory is ours, by the will of God...and God-willing things'll be good.

## Dreaming Civil Society

What was at stake for those who made the 25 January Revolution was not simply material or concrete. What they were contesting, as one observer acutely reported, was something decidedly "intangible."[14] It was a matter of hopes and ideals, of the values of autonomy and solidarity that define a more civil society.[15] An Egyptian activist recounted the story of the Tunisian fruit-seller whose martyrdom, in the twilight of 2010, had fired the democratic protest in the Arab Spring of early 2011. It had been a matter, he carefully explained, not of money but of individual "dignity."[16] Arrogant Tunisian officials had denied the street merchant a license, speaking "to him like he was a beggar."[17]

Neither was protest only an economic or material issue for the martyred Egyptian Khaled Said. It had been a civil matter, of chronic and flagrant official corruption, that moved him to rebel. The immensely influential Arabic Facebook page Wael Ghonim established in June 2010 to honor Said – 'We Are All Khaled Said' (WAAKS) – was filled with video clips and newspaper articles about police violence, official corruption, and the regime's distorted media of communication. "This is your country," Ghonim insisted to his followers, "a government official is your employee who gets his salary from your tax money, and you have rights."[18] In a 27 January posting, Ghonim wrote about "Freedom *and* the Loaf," the latter referring to bread, the former to moral aspiration, and he added, as if to clarify:

مطلب كل مصر شرف

All of Egypt is demanding honor/virtue.[19]

Five days later, one week into the January struggle, WAAKS (English) announced the "Egyptians [sic] Dignity Revolution,"[20] and six days after that proclaimed: "This is not a political revolution. This is not a religious revolution. This is an all Egyptians [sic] revolution. This is the dignity and freedom revolution."[21] Interviewed by Al Jazeera (English-language version), a demonstrator named Mohammed explained, "We are prepared to live on the bare minimum, as long as we feel like we have our dignity, that we are walking down the streets with our dignity."[22] According to an editorial in Le Monde, the Egyptian people were saying "no to misery and corruption and yes to dignity and freedom."[23] Mahmoud Gouda, a Cairo sales director, remembered how his brother had been tortured by Egyptian police: "In the name of my brother's dignity, I now demand the departure of Mubarak."[24] Shadia Abdelrahim, a twenty-six-year-old Cairo doctor repeated a similar idea: "It isn't a question of politics, but of dignity."[25] According to the Guardian, "the Egyptian regime has deprived the people of everything, including freedom and dignity, and has failed to supply them with their daily needs."[26] La Repubblica agreed: "They ask for bread, work, justice and dignity."[27] In the days after the government's most extreme effort at repressing the revolution, a New York Times reporter observed that "dignity" was "a word often used."[28]

Individual freedom and dignity depend upon the existence of a certain kind of community, one that is civil rather than primordial. A New Jersey man asked in a letter to the *New York Times*: "Is it possible that those who believe that every Muslim could be a terrorist might now at least be wondering if the Middle East is populated by people craving what all of us want, a world built upon basic freedoms with respect for divergent views?"[29] One of the organizations leading the Egyptian revolution, the April 6 Youth Movement, declared on its Arabic website that it was not sectional or individual interests, but a shared commitment to reconstructing a beloved community that drove the revolution: "Nothing brings us together except our love for this country and the desire to reform it."[30] Day after day, the revolutionaries represented themselves as a cross-section of Egyptian society, as weaving together a community that was universalistic in the most expansive and idealized sense. "The reality that emerged from interviews with protestors," the *New York Times* reported after the first day of agitation, was that "opposition to Mr. Mubarak's rule spreads across ideological lines [and] came from all social classes," that the protestors "did not belong to any particular group," and that many "were attending their first demonstration."[31] Lowly Egyptian foot soldiers declared, "this is the revolution of all the people."[32] Wealthy Egyptians, while acknowledging that "elites like us will say, 'Oh, we're going to lose out,'" insisted "we may have to lose out in order to give something back to ourselves."[33]

In the extraordinarily stratified context of contemporary Egypt, such observations elicited continual surprise. That participants in the revolution were motivated by a broadly encompassing, civil and universalistic solidarity, rather than by narrower, primordial, and more particularistic concerns, was a central motif of the *New York Times'* coverage over the movement's eighteen days:

> Friday's protest was the largest and most diverse yet, including young and old, women with Louis Vuitton bags and men in galabeyas, factory workers and film stars.[34]

> Hopes of Egyptians, Poor and Wealthy, Converge in Fight for Cairo Bridge.[35]

> The protestors came from every social class and included even wealthy Egyptians who are often dismissed as apolitical, or too comfortable to mobilize. For some of them in the crowd on Friday, the brutality of the security forces was a revelation. "Dogs!" they yelled at the riot police, as they saw bloodied protesters dragged away. "These people are Egyptians!"[36]

> There seemed to be a simple national consensus, felt by car mechanics in Upper Egypt and the café society in Cairo: the government has failed them.[37]

> Over the last several days, hundreds of thousands of Egyptians – from indigent fruit peddlers and doormen to students and engineers, even wealthy landlords – poured into the streets together.[38]

> Most of the week's protests appeared to represent a nearly universal cross section of the public.[39]

> The battle was waged by Mohammed Gamil, a dentist in a blue tie who ran toward the barricades of Tahrir Square. It was joined by Fayeqa Hussein, a veiled mother of seven who filled a Styrofoam container with rocks. Magdi Abdel-Rahman, a 60-year-old grandfather, kissed the ground before throwing himself against crowds [and] the charge was led by Yasser Hamdi, who said his 2-year-old daughter would live a life better than the one he endured. "Aren't you men?" he shouted. "Let's go!"[40]

> The uprising [was] the last option for not only the young
> and dispossessed but also virtually every element of Egypt's
> population – turbaned clerics, businessmen from wealthy
> suburbs, film directors and well-to-do engineers.[41]

Such observations were hardly confined to correspondents and columnists from the American paper. That the solidarity driving the revolution was civil and expansive was noted far and wide. An Al Jazeera (English) correspondent observed that "the people we have seen taking to the streets today are not the 50 or 60 activists that we have been seeing protesting in Egypt for the past five or six years," but "normal Egyptians, older women, younger men, even children."[42] A comment on its English website insisted:

> The pro-democracy protest in Tahrir Square was the most
> diverse gathering that I have ever witnessed in Egypt ... There
> were plenty of mid-teens to early 30s men and women in
> the pro-democracy camp. But with them were children, the
> elderly, the ultra-pious and the slickest cosmopolitans, workers,
> farmers, professionals, intellectuals, artists, long-time activists,
> complete neophytes to political protest, and representatives of
> all political persuasions.[43]

The *Guardian* reported on "an unlikely alliance of youth activists, political Islamists, industrial workers and football fans"[44] and that:

> Young people of every background and social class marched
> and sang together. Older, respected figures went round with
> food and blankets. Cigarette-smoking women in jeans sat next
> to their niqab-wearing sisters on the pavement. Old comrades
> from the student movement of the 1970s met for the first time

in decades. Young people went round collecting litter. People who stayed at home phoned nearby restaurants with orders to deliver food to the protesters. Not one religious or sectarian slogan was heard. The solidarity was palpable. And if this sounds romantic, well, it was and is.[45]

*La Repubblica* reminded its readers that Egypt's civic tradition was older than Italy's: "We understand more that Egyptians are beginning to think of their Muslim faith as secondary in respect to their political convictions, just as they have in history ... Egypt had a parliament four years before Italy."[46]

On the third day of revolution, Wael Ghonim underscored the civil nature of solidarity on WAAKS:

الكنيسة المصرية تجعو المسيحيين لحضور المظاهرات السلمية مع إخوتهم المسلمين ... الحمد لله و كلنا ايد واحدة لأن كلنا عايزين حقوقنا.

The Egyptian church invites Christians to attend peaceful demonstrations with their Muslim brothers ... Praise God and we all are supported as one for we all desire our rights.[47]

On the following day, this message went out on WAAKS (English): "For our brothers and sisters in Egypt. The winds of change are blowing – all Egyptians – Christians, Muslims, Everyone ... are together as one" (28 January 2011). Two days before, as the movement prepared for its first mass confrontation, Ghonim had declared a similar theme on WAAKS (Arabic):

سنخرج بمسيرات في كل مساجد وكنائس مصر الكبرى متجهين ناحية الميادين العامة ومعتصمين حتى ننال حقوقنا المسلوبة.

مصر ستخرج مسلميها ومسيحييها من أجل محاربة الفساد
والبطالة والظلم وغياب الحرية. سيتم تحديد المساجد والكنائس
ليلة الخميس.

We will exit into marches in all the great mosques and churches of Egypt heading towards public squares and staying until we receive our denied rights. Egypt will exit, its Muslims and its Christians, to fight corruption, unemployment, injustice, and the absence of freedom. Chosen churches and mosques will be announced Thursday night.[48]

From the first day of the uprising, revolutionary leaders presented themselves and their organizations as providing an impermeable shield around the emerging civil sphere of the nation, one that would protect not only the individual but the broader community upon which individuality depends. Warning that "abuse of any individual is against the entire nation," the April 6 Youth Movement warned the regime that, in the event of such abuse, "unforeseen results will come that cannot be controlled."[49]

**Quotes from Al Jazeera**

وأضاف البيان -الذي تلقت الجزيرة نت نسخة منه- أن
الحركة ستتخذ التدابير اللازمة لحماية الجميع قدر المستطاع،
وقالت "قمنا بتجهيز دروع واقية وكذلك أطباء وصيادلة
لإسعاف أي مواطن قد يتعرض لإيذاء جسدي...

The statement [by April 6 Youth Movement] – a copy of
which was received by Al Jazeera Net – added that the
movement will adopt necessary measures to protect
everyone to the best of its ability, and it said, "We have
employed protective shields as well as doctors and
pharmacists" to rescue any citizen that may be exposed to
physical harm.

ووصفت الحركة تصريحات وزارة الداخلية المصرية -التي
قالت فيها إنها ستتصدى بكل حزم للمظاهرة- بأنها
"متغطرسة وليست جديدة، فالحكومة تأبى إعطاء التصاريح
اللازمة، ثم تتعامل بطريقة قمعية مع الجماهير بحجة عدم
الحصول على تصريح بالمظاهرة.

The movement described the statements of the Interior
Ministry – that said that the ministry would address/thwart
any determination to protest – as "arrogant and nothing
new, the government refuses to give the necessary permits,
then deals repressively with the masses under the pretext of
failing to obtain permits for a protest."[50]

## Cultural Background: Binary Moral Classifications

For participants and observers alike, revolutionary conflicts are experienced as a life and death struggle between not just social groups but social representations, one representing the sacred, the other profane. A *Guardian* writer called the Egyptian regime "a quagmire of tyranny."[51] "This is a titanic struggle," one *New York Times* columnist reported during the uprising's final days, "between the tired but still powerful, top down 1952 Egyptian Army-led revolution and a new vibrant, but chaotic, 2011 people-led revolution from the bottom up."[52] Another *Times* columnist declared: "Rarely have we seen such epic clashes between the forces of light and darkness."[53]

For the Egyptian state and its ideological apparatus – Mubarak's secret police, his corrupt administration, puppet parliament, and house intellectuals – the events of the eighteen-day revolution, and the actors who drove them, were represented as deeply polluting; they were constructed by a negative discourse that legitimated, in fact demanded, their repression.[54] After the assassination of Anwar Sadat, Mubarak had projected a progressive narrative. Against the forces of fundamentalism, violence, and reaction, he would modernize Egypt and bring it into the future. "We will embark on our great path," he promised in his 1981 inaugural speech, "not stopping or hesitating, building and not destroying, protecting and not threatening, preserving and not squandering."[55] During the 1990s, fighting a low-level war against Islamist groups, Mubarak's regime represented itself, not only as the guarantor of social order, but also as the defender of modernity and even democratic reform, as working against the anti-democratic character of the Islamicist side.[56] A leading intellectual whom Mubarak appointed general secretary of the Supreme Council of Culture, for example, authored books with such titles as *Defending Enlightenment* and *Against Fanaticism*.[57] In 2006, even as Mubarak announced he would retain his presidency for life, he framed his decision in a progressive manner, promising the Parliament, "I will pursue with you the march of transition into the future, shouldering the responsibility and burdens as long as I draw breath."[58]

Such rhetoric would seem to defy the natural laws of social realism, but five years later Mubarak applied the same binary grid of moral signifiers to the signifieds of the 25 January Revolution. Those opposing the regime were "instigators," "foreigners" and "spies," not true "Egyptians," not the sincere "patriots" who constituted the "vast majority." While outside agitators engaged in "sabotage" and created "chaos," the state would maintain "stability" and "security." The street activists were a small "minority" of "outlaws," an "illegitimate and illegitimate" group who employed "force." The state, by contrast, was lawful, had "the popular support of the vast majority," and displayed an "ability to listen." Critics engaged in "propaganda," but Mubarak's regime was "careful" and "deliberate," willing to initiate "dialogue." The revolutionaries, by contrast, were taking "uncalculated and hasty steps that would produce more irrationality." They were "intellectual adolescents" with "little standing," while the state was "big" and "strong." The protests were quickly becoming "exhausted," even as Mubarak and his regime remained "resilient." Those who challenged the government were "dangerous," but the regime was "safe."[59]

*Table 1*   The Mubarak Regime's Classifications

| Profane Protest | Sacred Regime |
| --- | --- |
| Instigators | Egyptians |
| Foreigners, Spies | Patriots |
| Chaos | Security, Stability |
| Force | Willingness to listen |
| Hasty | Careful |
| Uncalculated | Deliberate |
| Irrational | Dialogue |
| Minority | Popular majority |
| Exhausted | Resilient |
| Little Standing | Big Strong |
| Dangerous | Safe |
| Primitive | Modern |
| Sectarian | Rational |
| Illegitimate | |
| Illegal | |
| Outlaws | |
| Sabotage | |
| Propaganda | |
| Intellectual adolescents | |

While there is evidence that Egyptian elites and masses initially had evinced some sympathy for such regime coding, as Mubarak's reign lengthened and his emergency decrees remained in place, his shaky connection to the collective consciousness faded along with his promises of modernization. Until the 25 January outbreak, however, there had been scarcely any public opportunity to articulate an alternative symbolic system, one that matched the regime's secularism and went toe-to-toe with it in a morally agonistic way. Demonstrations such as the Cairo Spring of 2005 and the 2008 food riots in El-Mahalla el-Kubra had been summarily quashed.[60] By contrast, from the beginning of the 25 January Revolution, protestors were able to seize the public stage, and they broadcast an alternative symbolic classification. Their moral categories were not, in themselves, sharply divergent from the ones that Mubarak himself employed. What changed was the relative weighting of one quality over another, and how these discursive signifiers were socially applied. Democracy and freedom became much more prominent, the state pushed over to the polluted side. Revolutionary discourse also found fresh tropes for speaking the sacred and profane, and they were now able to perform them practically, in time and space, in extraordinarily effective ways.

Inside the sacred and profane classification of the revolutionaries, Mubarak was exercising "repression" and "brute force," while the demonstrators called for "freedom" and "communication." The revolutionaries denounced the "barbaric" Egyptian state headed by a "modern day Pharaoh," interpreting his moves as "carefully calibrated." They characterized their own movement, by contrast, as "leaderless," choosing time and again to emphasize the "spontaneous" character of their activities. While regime officials were "dogs" and "thugs," the protesters were described as "the people." Mubarak had launched a "crackdown" to "throttle" the people's voice with "violence," but protestors remained "courageous" and "undaunted," and their ambition said to be "communication." The "arrogant" autocrat addressed his subjects as "sons and daughters"; the revolutionaries spoke of one another as "citizens." The demonstrators were "youthful"; the regime was "petrified." Mubarak's was a "dictatorial" regime; the revolution demanded "democracy."[61]

***Table 2***  The Revolutionaries' Classifications

| Profane Regime | Sacred Protest |
|---|---|
| Repression | Freedom |
| Choking brute force | Communication |
| Modern day pharaoh | Leaderless |
| Carefully calibrated | Spontaneous |
| Petrified | Youth |
| Dogs, thugs | The people |
| Mubarak and cronies | Vast majority of Egypt |
| Sons and daughters | Citizens |
| Dictator | Democracy |
| Arrogant | |
| Violence | |

If the Egyptian revolutionaries could represent themselves so effectively inside this binary discourse of civil society – speaking fluently about their democratic motives, relations and imagined institutions – this was due in no small part to a broader intellectual revolution in Arab political life, a dramatic shift in the fundaments of political language that provided the background representations for contemporaries' public speech. In the decades preceding the events of 25 January, the vanguard of Arab political culture had changed. The post-colonial promises of militant Arab nationalism lost their luster,[62] and important currents inside political Islam were shifting. Debates about civil society and democracy permeated books, newspaper articles, magazines, websites and the talking heads and interviews on Al Jazeera TV. Some secular intellectuals became "court liberals" who projected democracy as a distant ideal but kept quiet about contemporary Arab regimes. Others went into internal or external exile; publicly attacked Arab authoritarianism; and stridently demanded immediate radical, democratic change.[63] Such core Islamic ideas as *hurriya* (freedom) were expanded from the religious into the political sphere, and shariah law and the Islamic idea of justice began to be interpreted in civil ways.[64] Despite fears among such conservative interpreters as *USA Today* – that the Muslim Brotherhood would assume leadership and that it would be a "calamity"[65] – other Western journalists recognized that Islamism was leavened with a "variety of positions," many of which were explicitly democratic:[66] "There are Orthodox and heretical Nasserites, communists, trade union Labor Party members, Labour Muslim, liberals ... and certainly there are Islamists, but split into factions, and certainly much more complicated than we imagine them to be."[67]

*La Repubblica* stressed the secular nature of the demonstrations:

> Yesterday, Friday, the day of prayer, the crowd chanted the usual cry of Allah'u Akhbar, Allah is great. But the slogan of the revolt, the one that filled the streets, is another: "Illegitimate!" Mubarak is an illegitimate president (because his election was a fraud).[68]

An Egyptian leader of the Muslim Brotherhood wrote a *New York Times* op-ed piece stressing this democratic turn in Arab and Muslim intellectual opinion in the present day:

> We envision the establishment of a democratic, civil state that
> draws on universal measures of freedom and justice, which
> are central Islamic values ... We embrace democracy not as a
> foreign concept ... but as a set of principles and objectives that
> are inherently compatible with and reinforce Islamic tenets.[69]

Nowhere was this Arab intellectual revolution more visible, and its effects more palpable, than in the coverage of the revolution that Al Jazeera television broadcast in Arabic to the Egyptian people and beyond. Its journalists and editors strongly identified with the activists' civil and democratic aspirations, and their reporting, while professional, often seemed to be speaking in the movement's name. On the first day of the uprising, 25 January, the Arabic network provided a framework for the events that identified the protestors as sacred carriers of honest and principled democratic activism, stigmatizing its regime opponents as arrogant, fraudulent, repressive, aggressive, and violent.

---

**Quotes from Al Jazeera**

حذرت حركة شباب 6 أبريل وزارة الداخلية المصرية من
التعامل بعنف مع النشطاء والمتظاهرين الذين سينزلون
إلى الشوارع اليوم في احتجاج يصادف يوم عيد الشرطة، في
الوقت الذي أنذرت فيه الحكومة المصرية المتظاهرين بأنهم
سيواجهون الاعتقال إن هم مضوا قدما في تنظيم الاحتجاجات.

The April 6 Youth Movement was warned by the Egyptian Interior ministry that it will deal violently with activists and protestors that will take to the streets today in a protest falling upon National Police Day [25 January], at a time that the Egyptian government warned protestors that they would face arrest if they went ahead in organizing the protests.

حذرت حركة شباب 6 أبريل وزارة الداخلية المصرية من التعامل بعنف مع النشطاء والمتظاهرين الذين سينزلون إلى وحذر بيان أصدرته الحركة وزارة الداخلية من ممارسة "الاحتيال القديم بدس عملائها من البلطجية داخل صفوف المتظاهرين لإحداث مشاجرات واعتداءات على الممتلكات العامة, ثم اتخاذ ذلك ذريعة لسحق المتظاهرين ونعتهم بالمخربين والخارجين على القانون".

And a statement issued by the April 6 Movement warned the Interior Ministry of its practice of "the old fraud of poking its clients, thugs, inside the ranks of the protestors in order to create fights and attacks on public property, taking that as a pretext for crushing the protestors, labeling them as vandals and outlaws."

وخاطب البيان قوات الأمن بأن "يلتزموا بحدود القانون"...

And the statement addressed the security forces to "commit themselves to the limits of the law" ...

ووصفت الحركة تصريحات وزارة الداخلية المصرية -التي قالت
فيها إنها ستتصدى بكل حزم للمظاهرة- بأنها "متغطرسة وليست
جديدة، فالحكومة تأبى إعطاء التصاريح اللازمة، ثم تتعامل بطريقة
قمعية مع الجماهير بحجة عدم الحصول على تصريح بالمظاهرة.

The movement described the statements of the Interior
Ministry – that said that the ministry would address/thwart
any determination to protest – as "arrogant and nothing
new, the government refuses to give the necessary permits,
then deals repressively with the masses under the pretext of
failing to obtain permits for a protest."[70]

For many Western observers, the intellectual revolution
in the Arab world was obscured by the anti-American and
anti-Zionist sentiments that often accompanied its fervent
expression, as well as by the violence of radical Islamic
fundamentalists that crystallized during the same period of
time. Writing about the 25 January Revolution, for example,
*USA Today* characterized the Muslim Brotherhood as "a banned
political movement that wants a government run strictly as an
Islamic state."[71] The impact of the Arab intellectual revolution
was obscured, as well, by the subtle power that long-lasting
dictatorships can exercise over the mentalities of those they
dominate, sometimes causing them to doubt their own
capacities for rule. Mohammed ElBaradei, the Nobel laureate
who had returned to Egypt to organize public opposition
against the Mubarak regime, observed that "people were

taught not to think or act,"[72] acknowledging "frankly, I didn't think people were ready."[73] Expressing surprise when members of the Egyptian elite participated in the demonstrations, one protestor commented, "This is the class that never spoke out before."[74]

The 25 January Revolution began when a people who had seemed an "apolitical and largely apathetic public" found their voice.[75] It was not only resistance to the state's physical repression that propelled and sustained the rebellion, but outrage against a regime discourse that polluted the Egyptian people as abject and its activists as evil. Because social signification is arbitrary and socially constructed, it is always in play. Binary moral classification may seem static, but it is not. Its social anchoring is restless and undecided, its interpretation dynamic and potentially explosive. Binary structures pollute those who may think of themselves as sacred, and purify those who others passionately judge to be profane. As "25 January" gained momentum, the movement became ever more strenuously subject to depredations from the regime's polluting symbols, and indignation at such humiliating misapprehension increased in kind. "A people who once complained of their quiescence," the New York Times observed, "would no longer stay quiet." It was because they finally could speak that "they seized control of their lives."[76] In the process, Al Jazeera (Arabic) reported, "the Egyptians in the street surprised observers and analysts [and] the Egyptian president and government," and "they surprised even themselves."[77]

*Table 3*   Tension between Moral Antinomies

| Mubarak Classification | | Revolutionary Classification | |
|---|---|---|---|
| Profane Protest | Sacred Regime | Profane Regime | Sacred Protest |
| Instigators | Egyptians | Repression | Freedom |
| Foreigners, spies | Patriots | Choking brute force | Communication |
| Chaos | Security, stability | Modern day pharaoh | Leaderless |
| Force | Willingness to listen | Carefully calibrated | Spontaneous |
| Hasty | Careful | Petrified | Youth |
| Uncalculated | Deliberate | Dogs, thugs | The people |
| Irrational | Dialogue | Mubarak and cronies | Vast majority of Egypt |
| Minority | Popular majority | Sons and daughters | Citizens |
| Exhausted | Resilient | Dictator | Democracy |
| Little standing | Big, strong | Arrogant | |
| Dangerous | Safe | Violence | |
| Primitive | Modern | | |
| Sectarian | Rational | | |
| Illegitimate | | | |
| Illegal | | | |
| Outlaws | | | |
| Sabotage | | | |
| Propaganda | | | |
| Intellectual adolescents | | | |

# Narratives of National Decline and Salvation

Much as counterpoint propels baroque music, the agonism of juxtaposed moral codes energizes revolutions. The protestors of 25 January aimed to purify themselves and pollute the regime engaged in their moral depredation. In order to do so, they folded the morally charged binaries into a temporal language of before and after, a narrative organized by conflict between social actors who represented their respective moral sides. The revolutionary narrative inscribed the unfolding events of democratic insurgency inside a plot of national decline and resurrection. There was broad and fervent idealization of the Egypt of old. Once, Egypt had been a great nation and civilization. Despite some imprecision about the beginning of the golden age, the date of Egypt's decline is clear: it was during Mubarak's reign. "All Egyptian people believe that their country is a great country with very deep roots in history," a Cairo University professor explained, "but the Mubarak regime broke our dignity in the Arab world and in the whole world."[78] When the Associated Press interviewed Ismail Syed, the hotel worker allowed, "this is the first time I am protesting, but we have been a cowardly nation. We have to finally say no."[79] Mohammed ElBaradei lamented that "Egypt, the land of the Library of Alexandria, of a culture that contributed groundbreaking advances in mathematics, medicine, and science, has fallen far behind."[80] A protestor in the street put it more simply: "I want to say this to the regime: Thirty years is more than enough. Our country is going down and down because of your policies."[81] Many other revolutionaries expressed the same sentiment: "For thirty years, Egypt lost its place. We've been ruled by mercenaries and rulers who stole from our treasuries. It's over now, the people have woken up, and they're going to rise again. Egypt is going to be the example again."[82] As a coffee-shop owner joined protesters in Shubra, northern Cairo, he shouted, "Egypt is waking up."[83] In the early morning of 27 January, after the first days of successful mobilization and confrontation, Wael Ghonim rallied insurgent forces for more sacrifices in the days ahead. "We won't be intimidated," he tapped on WAAKS (Arabic):

كلنا سنموت لتحيا مصر

"We shall die for Egypt to live."[84]

A week later, Al Jazeera (Arabic) broadcast a segment called "Opinions of a number of Protesters in Tahrir Square"

–أراء عدد من المعتصمين في ميدان التحرير

*Figure 2*    Screenshot of women protestors from Al Jazeera

a series face-to-face interviews with fiercely determined protestors in Tahrir Square. An older woman in black in the entrance to a tent told the interviewer:

لو أعدنا سنة هنا لاحدي ما نأخذ هائنا عشنا كثير
محرومين و ذلنا بلدنا كثير.

Even If we stayed here for a whole year, we would stay until we get what is rightfully ours. We have lived for so long deprived and our country has been humiliated very much.

A woman carrying an Egyptian flag declared:

إن شاء الله هنأخذ هريتنا و نحرر مصر من ظلم حسني مبارك.

God willing we shall seize our freedom and free Egypt from the injustice/oppression of Hosni Mubarak.[85]

Journalists interpreted the revolutionary narration in the same way. According to the *New York Times*, Egypt was a "nation that once saw itself as the center of civilization and the Arab world,"[86] and it recorded "the country's erosion over decades of authoritarian rule," how it had "gone from being a cosmopolitan showcase to a poor, struggling city that evokes barely a vestige of its former grandeur."[87] Egypt had once been "the cradle of civilization and a one-time leader of the Arab world," but now it "had slipped towards backwardness and irrelevance."[88]

The lowest point in this inverted parabola was the present. Contemporary Egypt is narrated as the worst of times. A secular protest leader decried the "hell we are in right now."[89] A media advisor for the Muslim Brotherhood declared, "everyone is suffering from social problems, unemployment, inflation, corruption and oppression."[90] A popular playwright poeticized: "Every Egyptian is carrying inside of them 100 short stories of pain and novels of grievance."[91] The antagonist in this narrative of declension was clear: Mubarak was to blame. "This nightmare is the ruling party and the current regime," a former

Brotherhood member who had quit from frustration explained: "This is everyone's nightmare."[92] According to a former Egyptian political prisoner, the sociologist Saad Ibrahim:

> Those in Tahrir Square have had their fill of the pharaoh's deception ... This aging pharaoh is trying to create the false impression that without his steady hand, Egypt will descend into chaos. The carefully orchestrated and well-armed mobs of "pro-Mubarak demonstrators" are just the latest acts in his three decades of deception.[93]

The *Wall Street Journal* described how "two teenagers on a marble pedestal in the adjacent park held up a cardboard placard, as eloquent as it was blunt: 'Hosni Mubarak isn't president anymore. He is the Devil.'"[94] *La Repubblica* wrote, "The president is now a head without a future, a symbol, a shadow, embarrassing,"[95] describing Mubarak's failure to resign as "the final joke of a plastic pharaoh."[96]

The 25 January Revolution was a new plot line driven by world-transforming protagonists carrying on their shoulders hopes for national renewal. On the morning of the first day of the uprising, the April 6 Youth Movement warned security forces "to not exercise what was exercised before, because that time has already gone by and passed."[97] The *Guardian* documented the same national narrative in the streets.

> In the narrow side streets protesters regrouped, while well wishers on their balconies above threw down water for those with streaming eyes from the tear gas. "Wake up Egypt, your silence is killing us," came the yells from below. Others shouted: "Egyptians, come down to join us." Their appeals were answered with people streaming down from the apartment blocks: "We

are change" and "Gamal (Mubarak) tell your father Egyptians hate him," were the cries.[98]

Overthrowing the Mubarak regime would move Egypt from darkness to light. "There are a lot of things wrong with this country," an unemployed protestor remarked, explaining "the president has been here for thirty years."[99] *Le Monde* reported Muhammed ElBaradei's comment, upon his most recent return to Egypt: "This is a critical moment in the history of Egypt ... The will of change must be respected."[100] *La Repubblica*, headlined "El Baradei Man of Destiny 'Today a New Country is Born'."[101] Expelling Mubarak would push Egypt from one side to the other of the binary code. If successful, it would allow Egyptians to re-inscribe their nation on the sacred side. The regime and the protestors both loved the nation, but only one conceived this nationalism in a civil way.[102] The *New York Times* reported:[103]

> "This is our country," said Maram Jani, a 33-year old wearing a pink veil who returned after working as a psychologist for three years in the Persona Gulf. "We want to stay in our country. We want to share in its wealth, we want to be part of its land. They can only laugh at us so long, make fun of us for so long."[104]
>
> The atmosphere in Tahrir Square reverted from embattled to jubilant. The protesters abandoned their makeshift barriers to chant, pray and sing the national anthem around the center of the square.[105]
>
> "We took our freedom," Mustafa Abudrasheed Muhanna said. "Egypt is born again." So was the Egyptian flag, no longer seen as a symbol of a stagnant state, a bureaucrat's wall decoration or a backdrop for state television broadcasts of Mr. Mubarak's meetings. In the square on Friday, it was a woman's shawl,

a child's plaything and a cherished accessory. Sold for $2, it was marked in black pen with political slogans or signed like a yearbook. Everywhere, the flags waved … One sign held by a young man said: "Mubarak: Enter + Shift + Delete." Moawia Mohamed, 20, held another that said, "welcome to the New Egypt."[106]

Samar Ali, a twenty-three-year-old graduate of the University of Fine Arts in Cairo, recounted that, "I decided to go to Tahrir square," but "I was afraid of the Islamists or that I would be sexually harassed by the men in the street." What she found when she got to the square was a different Egypt, a country on the rise: "I was shocked to see that those Egyptians who made me so afraid are the ones who now protect me, with so much dignity. I discovered another Egypt, the one my father had told me about."[107]

Declaring that the demonstrators "broke the barrier of fear," novelist Alaa al-Aswany commented to Al Jazeera (English) that "the writers of the regime" have been "saying Egypt is not Tunisia and Egyptians are less educated than Tunisians." He countered: "Here is the thing: these young people proved they can take their rights forcefully."[108] Firas al-Atraqchi, a former Al Jazeera journalist, linked the revolution to national revival in the same way.

> In more than 18 years of living in Cairo, I have never felt the sense of excited hope that exists in Egypt tonight. From speaking to colleagues (many of whom are journalists covering the protests), friends and neighbours, they all feel that despite the number of teargas canisters fired at protesters and the number of those who have been beaten and detained, that a long-dormant patriotism and pride has been finally awakened.[109]

The BBC reported that, during the culminating demonstrations in Tahrir Square on 11 February, "three chants were dominant – and very telling."

> One – "Lift your head up high, you're Egyptian" – was a response to how humiliated, how hopeless we'd been made to feel over the last four decades. The second was: "We'll get married, We'll have kids," and reflected the hopes of the millions whose desperate need for jobs and homes had been driving them to risk their lives to illegally cross the sea to Europe or the desert to Libya. The third chant was: "Everyone who loves Egypt, come and rebuild Egypt."[110]

Revolution would resurrect Egypt's golden age. During one demonstration, activists distributed a fake version of *Al Ahram*, the state-owned newspaper. On its front page was a picture of a mummy from the pharaonic days. The text below read: "To the grandchildren of our grandchildren in Tahrir Square. You gave me back my spirit."[111]

## The Script and the Carrier Group

These were the collective representations that formed the background for the revolutionary upheaval in Egypt – its moralizing binaries, energizing narratives, and intellectual antecedents.[112] The upheaval that became the 25 January Revolution began as an effort to perform these background representations, to move from symbolic construction to symbolic action. For the collective action to succeed, symbols had to be projected from their creators to layered audiences: to gather followers and foot soldiers from the more committed; to engage the elites; to seduce the middle; and to gain attention outside, from the Arab region and the global civil sphere.

The agents who were at the core of this performative project formed the revolution's "carrier group." It was they who projected the symbols and, after they made the connection with audiences, directed the revolutionary *mise en scène*. The "scene" of the revolutionary drama was peopled by the hundreds of thousands of protestors, but this unfolding *mise en scène* was directed, not by the mass of people, but by movement intellectuals[113] who tried to work out the script and choreograph street actions in advance.

Because the mere existence of such a directorate, even a relatively loosely organized one, seemed threatening to the revolution's representation as democratic, its leaders tried to keep their strategizing invisible and their very existence under wraps. The first media mentions of a revolutionary directorate did not surface in the Western media until nearly a week after the movement began. Despite claims of being spontaneous and leaderless, it was reported that, not only throughout the events but well before them, "a small group of Internet-savvy young political organizers" had been meeting frequently with one another. On Sunday, 30 January, for example, overlapping members of the leadership network reconnoitered at three different times and locations. Every evening, leaders would prepare a blueprint for the next day's events.[114] Distributed the next morning via email and text message, and updated throughout the day, the script provided slogans, suggested routes and movements, and assigned key actors roles to play and words to say.[115]

Organizers used photocopies to disseminate information. Anonymous leaflets circulating in Cairo ... provide practical and tactical advice for mass demonstrations, confronting riot police, and besieging and taking control of government offices. Signed "long live Egypt," the slickly produced 26-page document calls on demonstrators to begin with peaceful protests, carrying roses but no banners, and march on official buildings while persuading policemen and soldiers to join their ranks. The leaflet asks recipients to redistribute it by email and photocopy, but not to use social media such as Facebook and Twitter, which are being monitored by the security forces. Protesters in Cairo are advised to gather in large numbers in their own neighbourhoods away from police and troops and then move towards key installations such as the state broadcasting HQ on the Nile-side Corniche and try to take control "in the name of the people." Other priority targets are the presidential palace and police stations in several parts of central Cairo. The leaflet includes aerial photographs with approach routes marked and diagrams on crowd formations. Suggested "positive" slogans include "long live Egypt" and "down with the corrupt regime." There are no signs of slogans reflecting the agenda of the powerful Muslim Brotherhood. It advises demonstrators to wear clothing such as hooded jackets, running shoes, goggles and scarves to protect against teargas, and to carry dustbin lids – to ward off baton blows and rubber bullets – first aid kits, and roses to symbolise their peaceful intentions. Diagrams show how to defend against riot police and push in waves to break through their ranks. "The most important thing is to protect each other," the leaflet says.[116]

Even after older and more established opposition leaders joined the insurrection, it was these "young internet pioneers" who were "still calling the shots," and who remained "the vanguard behind the scenes."[117] At the end of the eighteen days of protest, the *New York Times* headlined: "Wired, Educated, and Shrewd, Young Egyptians Guide Revolt."[118]

Stories about the young leadership network emerged in bits and pieces over the course of the revolution's second and third weeks: revelations about their friendships, backgrounds, and ambitions, how they had met, their organizing history, and the roles they now played. Their identities, interests, and solidarity were typically described from a materialist perspective, as those of a new class[119] whose technological labor and higher education inscribed in them a critical orientation[120] that they could now put on display.[121] It seems clear, however, that the revolutionary leadership was much more and much less than that. Their day jobs were many and varied. Some worked in high-tech, but others were full-time political organizers; some ran NGOs; others were feminist and labor activists; some had businesses; others were religious leaders. In fact, the only demographic they did share was their relative youth. They were truly a "carrier" group – for the Arab intellectual revolution, for the moral binaries of civil society, and for the narrative of national resurrection that would save the Egyptian nation from further decline. It was shared ideas that brought this group together, cultural perceptions forged from the searing heat of common experiences and propelled by an uncommon willingness to sacrifice their privileges for some greater good.

The collective identity of these youthful activists was "years in the making,"[122] transforming the nascent carrier group from more traditional, working-class oriented activists into radical advocates for civil society.[123] Their loose association began with the "*Kefaya*" (Enough) movement in 2005, and the "Youth for Change" brigade they organized within it landed many in prison. By 2008, many had retreated to their computers, becoming politicized bloggers calling for a wave of anti-regime strikes. They set up their first Facebook page to promote the Mahala protest in March 2008. In the face of the violent repression of workers and their families, some youthful activists formed the April 6 Youth Movement and went back to the drawing board. Under the influence not only of their practical experience but surging intellectual interest in civil society, the revolutionaries began reading up on strategic non-violence, particularly the ideas of Gene Sharpe, the American whose philosophy of radical civil protest derived from Mahatma Gandhi and Martin Luther King and whose strategic thinking had inspired the Serbian youth group Otpor's struggle against Slobodan Milošević. Some Egyptian activists actually travelled to Serbia for political re-education; others set up an organization called the Academy of Change in Qatar to promote Sharpe's ideas.[124] "The Academy of Change is sort of like our Marx and we are like Lenin," a youthful member of the leadership group offered during the events of 25 January. Days before the 25 January Revolution, organizers from both Serbia and the Egyptian Academy of Change helped the directorate to train protest organizers in Cairo.[125] They were intent on teaching activists to resolutely maintain non-violence; otherwise, it would become impossible to perform a democratic civil sphere. As the first day's demonstrations began, the WAAKS (English) administrator made these commitments strikingly clear.

Some members believe that a peaceful protest in Egypt will
not do much. All our protests are peaceful and legal ones.
If you have a different opinion please feel free to say it,
but I have never and will never call for or support a protest
anywhere unless it is 100% legal and peaceful. (18 January 2011,
12.15 p.m.)

## Struggle and *Mise en Scène*

Social performances have many elements, each necessary but
none by itself sufficient. Revolutions need carrier groups, and
these groups make every effort to compose compelling scripts.
The next step is to make the scripts walk and talk. Walking and
talking means putting a script into practice, creating actual
events, with real human beings, which unfolds in time and
space. Social dramas, unlike theatrical ones, are open-ended
and contingent. They can be staged, but nobody is certain
whether the actors will arrive, who they will be, how events
will unfold, which side will win a confrontation, and what the
drama's effects on the audience will be. In relatively democratic
societies, where there exists some independence for the civil
sphere, the effect of political performance is contingent,
but its staging and dramatization – the walking and talking
of scripted action – is not particularly difficult to pull off. In
more repressive societies, where civil spheres are suppressed,
performative success must be measured more minimally.
In some real part, an opposition performance is successful
merely by the fact of its having taken place. Autocracies aim
to prevent oppositional political performances from ever

occurring. It is in order to block the transition from scripting to walking and talking that the regime puts its threats of dire punishment into place – from the destruction of life routines to imprisonment, torture, and death. Simply to stage a public performance in a repressive society is already an achievement. It marks its effect, as John Austin might have said, in the very act of its own doing: from being merely words with meanings, opposition becomes words that do things.[126] Meanings are instantiated in time and place, and the symbols signifying a situation move from the subjunctive to present tense.[127]

One of the best ways to stop public performances, to keep organizers from being able to do things with words, is to prevent those staging opposition from communicating with others who might wish to attend. Without the means of symbolic production, communication beyond immediate face-to-face contact becomes impossible. Even as the Mubarak regime monopolized and manipulated print and television media, its insistent investment in a progressive, modernizing narrative compelled it to be thoroughly "wired" at the same time. Some twenty million of Egypt's eighty million population owned computers or social networking devices, guaranteeing regular access to the World Wide Web. In 2006, the Mubarak government proudly hosted Wikipedia's annual global convention.

This paradoxical wiring of the nation presented an Achilles heel to which the carrier group of Egyptian dissidents took careful aim. In early 2010, the group was joined by Wael Ghonim, a thirty-one-year-old Google executive who had been part of the circle around Mohammed ElBaradei. Director of the global internet company's marketing for North Africa and the Middle East, Ghonim was expert in techniques of symbolic projection, in moving a digital message from speaker to audience:[128] "I worked in marketing, and I knew that if you build a brand you get people to trust the brand."[129] Communicating with hundreds of thousands of WAAKS (Arabic) followers, Ghonim conducted online exercises in democratic participation, dress rehearsals for the uprising to come. After the victory of the Tunisian revolution on 14 January 2011, leaders sensed the time for performing mass public opposition had finally arrived. If 50,000 persons signed up, the Facebook page messaged, the first public protest would be staged. More than 100,000 responded. 25 January was Police Day, a national holiday honoring a police revolt suppressed by the British colonialists. The carrier group transformed it into an uprising against the post-colonial state. Before launching a full-fledged demonstration, however, the organizers tried one more "out of town" run, to test how far into the layered audiences[130] their radical performance of opposition would reach.

> When the 25th came, the coalition of young activists, almost all of them affluent, wanted to tap into the widespread frustration with the country's autocracy, and also the grinding poverty of Egyptian life. They started by trying to rally poor people with complaints about pocketbook issues: "They are eating pigeon and chicken, but we eat beans every day."[131]

Marching through the narrow streets and alleys of working-class Cairo, the organizers discovered an extraordinary response. Egyptians leaned out of windows shouting encouragement, banging pots and pans in support. Thousands left their apartments and poured into the streets to join the demonstration.[132] Two of Mubarak's National Party buildings were set on fire. Placing a call to his fellow organizers who had gathered to await the results of this trial run, Ghonim reported it a massive success. The carrier group now had clear evidence that their movement could connect a wider audience.

The revolution could begin. Routes to Tahrir Square were chosen, street leaders assigned, and a massive, public, aggressive yet insistently non-violent confrontation with the autocratic state began later that day. "Freedom, Freedom, Freedom," the swelling crowds chanted, as they coursed through the streets on their way to Tahrir (Liberation) Square.[133] As the demonstration built on 25 January, a series of postings on WAAKS (English) juxtaposed the protest drama's sacred civil purpose with the profane, anti-democratic response of the regime.

> Protesters at the High Court break down the Police siege and run towards Tahrir square. (1.23 p.m.)
>
> Protesters moving to opera house from tahrir square. Their number is well over 1000. (1.38 p.m.)
>
> Police moved in on protesters and attacking protesters badly. Using batons and water cannons. (3.50 p.m.)
>
> Confirmed: Tahrir Square is now COMPLETELY ours. Egyptian Police now is only worried about protecting their head quarters: Ministry of interior. (4.55 p.m.)
>
> BREAKING NEWS: Police in Egypt open fire on protesters ... Our correspondent was hit in his head ... with rubber bullets. (6.12 p.m., 6.19 p.m.)

> Confirmed reports: Restaurants in Tahrir square are giving away
> food for free to protesters. What more are you waiting for to go
> to join your fellow country men in Tahrir? You'll get a free meal
> at least!:) (8.39 p.m.)
>
> For all Egyptians: Twitter is closed as you know, Facebook will
> close very soon. Please All use proxies and tell ALL your friends
> in Egypt to use proxy to connect. (11.29 p.m.)

By the end of that 25 January evening, the carrier group knew that they had been able to make their script walk and talk. The closest rows of layered audiences had identified with the leaders' performance. An Egyptian observer reported how, on the first day of the demonstrations, the once disparate organizing groups had "fused, and with them multitudes of Egyptians young and old":

> For Cairo they chose three locations: Shubra, Matariyya and
> Arab League Street. These were strategic choices: naturally
> crowded neighbourhoods, with lots of side streets. Young
> activists started their march in nearby areas, collected a
> following and by the time they reached, for example, Arab
> League Street, they were 20,000 marching. The Central Security
> Forces were in chaos; when they formed cordons the people
> just broke through them. When they raised their riot shields and
> batons the young people walked right up to them with their
> hands up chanting "Silmiyyah! ( Peaceful) Silmiyyah!"[134]

These early responders to the revolution would now become part of a newly enlarged collective actor, forming a massive social movement that, over the next seventeen days, would battle Mubarak and his state for performative success.

From that afternoon forward, what the carrier group

directed, and the expanding Egyptian participant-audience enacted, was a gradually ascending, day-after-day drama of good challenging evil, of an outraged but peaceful community of citizen-activists who had the courage not only to keep demonstrating and speaking for democracy, but to die for it. The size and enthusiasm waxed and waned over the eighteen days, but the slope was upward. Gradually, and seemingly inevitably, the emotional weighting of the sacred revolutionary drama increased. On 23 January, journalists had predicted the imminent demonstrations would mark the beginning of a "political evolution."[135] Political experts cautioned, however, against an analogy with the anti-communist democratic uprisings of 1989. After listing the ways that the Jasmine revolution in Tunisia must be considered unique, one neo-conservative intellectual remarked: "There are plenty of reasons to think we are not on the cusp of a democratic avalanche."[136] Three days later, the media were reporting that "tens of thousands" of demonstrators had "filled the streets" in "the largest display of popular dissatisfaction since the bread riots of 1977,"[137] and that, "as evening fell, thousands of people converged on Tahrir Square, in the centre of Cairo, and began an occupation."[138] Six days later: "Egypt quakes beneath the fury of a huge public uprising."[139] Three days after that, journalists reported that, "from the perspective of the protestors and many others ... the uprising had become what they called a 'popular revolution',"[140] and a blogger for the *Guardian* proclaimed, "we are witnessing a true revolution."[141] The next day it was declared "one of the most spectacular popular movements in Egypt's history."[142] As one of the youthful organizers, Salma Said, told

*USA Today*, the growing scale was such that the organizers had to turn to "young Cairo soccer fans to help them organize against police actions," because they "had experience with unruly mobs and police."[143]

The denotative content of the demonstrators' chants and placards was clear. They called on their fellow members of the national community to join them in their civil crusade and for the dangerously anti-democratic regime on the other side to resign.

> Where are all the Egyptian people?![144]
>
> People, people, take to the streets.[145]
>
> Tomorrow all the Egyptians are going to be in the streets.[146]
>
> Mubarak, your plane is waiting.[147]
>
> Game over Mubarak! Democracy now![148]

But it was the emotional and symbolic connotations of the swelling streams of movement and confrontation that also mattered, not only their literal messages. What was unfolding before the layered audience, both near and far, was an extraordinary social drama. Participants and observers alike evoked the language of theatre. In the midst of the first afternoon's march, WAAKS (English) tapped, "Amazing scenes," (25 January 1.23 p.m.), a phrase echoed in the *Guardian*.[149] Journalists described the revolutionary demonstrations as tableaux – a "day of drama,"[150] "the Egyptian Drama,"[151] and "Thursday's drama."[152] And they, too, recorded the "remarkable scenes"[153] and "dramatic scenes."[154]

The revolutionary performances spread to several Egyptian cities but they were concentrated in Cairo's Tahrir Square, the geographical center of Egypt's capital city that now became its symbolic center as well. The *Guardian* described the square as the "scene of the ongoing mass demonstrations,"[155] and the *Wall Street Journal* suggested the revolt "had found a stage worthy of its ambitions."[156] The revolutionary *mise en scène* consisted largely of marches into and out of the square, speeches and demonstrations inside it, and pitched battles to retain control of this physical-cum-symbolic stage. Dramas rolled across this stage hour after hour, day after day, evening after evening, and they became riveting public events.

A compelling plot needs twists and turns, so that audiences are on the edge of their seats and never know what's next. Suspense rivets attention. "The Drama in Egypt: What Is the Next Act?," the *New York Times* headlined in its letters section at the drama's halfway point, on 4 February.[157] That same day, its news columns reported that "control of the streets" had "cycled through a dizzying succession of stages."[158] Reporters narrated day-to-day events as a plot filled with suspenseful twists and turns:

> 25 January: Zeinab Mohamed, an Egyptian blogger, commented, "I got a Facebook invitation for the 25 January, 'Anger' day, at the same time I was covering the Tunisian revolution ... I felt they were overestimating the situation: revolutions do not happen on Facebook or on a specific date. I thought it would be just another day of small protests downtown where protesters are harassed by the security forces as usual. But how wrong I was."[159]
>
> 26 January: It was not clear whether the size and intensity of the demonstrations ... would or could be sustained.[160]
>
> 28 January: The government seems to be using a version of a

rope-a-dope strategy Muhammad Ali used to defeat George Foreman in 1974. Mr. Ali spent round after round against the ropes as Mr. Foreman pounded himself into exhaustion.[161]

29 January: The crisis in Egypt has reached a critical turning point.[162]

Even as armored military vehicles deployed around important Egyptian government institutions on Friday for the first time in decades, it remained difficult to predict what role the armed forces might play in either quelling the disturbances or easing President Hosni Mubarak from power.[163]

"We don't know if the army is with us or against us."[164]

Revolution, transition, coup? Whatever the outcome of the chaos which was rampant yesterday in the streets of Cairo, one thing is clear, Egypt will never be the same.[165]

30 January: "The president is ... on shaky ground [and] he doesn't know what will happen tomorrow."[166]

There is a current of anxiety over what the protests would lead to.[167]

No one seemed sure where the movement would lead.[168]

2 February: "It is not possible to say what will happen next. Everything is up in the air."[169]

4 February: The momentum of the opposition movement has ebbed and flowed.[170]

5 February: Egypt's revolution is far from decided.[171]

7 February: "It's exciting but also a little bit scary ... People are getting hurt and also, I don't know what will happen next."[172]

8 February: It is not easy to predict what will happen next in Egypt's uprising.[173]

Momentum has seemed to shift by the day in a climactic struggle.[174]

Protesters and the government are locked in a battle for momentum.[175]

12 February: We are a long way from knowing how Egypt will turn out.[176]

As events zigzagged forth and back, journalists narrated the pulsating uncertainty as a sequence of chapters, numbered by the week and day.

"This is the first day of the Egyptian revolution," said Karim Rizk, at one of the Cairo rallies.[177]

The six day old protest here entered a new stage.[178]

On Tuesday, the eighth day of demonstrations, hundreds of thousands went to Liberation Square.[179]

A dramatic eighth day of mass protests.[180]

Nine days after a diverse band of protestors mobilized on the Internet and gathered by the thousands.[181]

On the ninth day of the uprising …[182]

For eleven days … the dominating demand [has been] that Mubarak should go away.[183]

In the eleven days since the Cairo uprising began …[184]

The twelfth day of protest …[185]

Twelve days into an uprising in Egypt …[186]

As Egypt's revolt entered its third week …[187]

On the fifteenth day of protests …[188]

After seventeen days …[189]

Eighteen Days in Tahrir Square …[190]

In the most compelling dramatic plots, the contingent becomes the teleological. Strong narratives, *pace* Aristotle, must have not only a beginning and middle, but an end. The sense of an ending permeates the present, sustaining the protagonists in their struggle against evil others, propelling the densely organized action forward so that its meaning can be transformed on the other side. Even as they were engulfed in the anxiety of dramatic interaction, the revolutionary demonstrators believed they would ultimately triumph.

> "Our protest on the 25th is the beginning of the end," wrote organisers on the Arabic "We are all Khaled Said" Facebook group that day. "It is the end of silence, acquiescence and submission to what is happening in our country. It will be the start of a new page in Egypt's history, one of activism and demanding our rights."[191]

> After we walked from Tahrir Square across the Nile bridge, Professor Mamoun Fandy remarked to me that there is an old Egyptian poem that says: "The Nile can bend and turn, but what is impossible is that it would ever dry up." The same is true of the river of freedom that is loose here now. Maybe you can bend it for a while, or turn it, but it is not going to dry up.[192]

> A long dead North African poet's most famous poem has become the anthem of the movement. His work seems to define the protests and their ambitions ... "If one day, a people desires to live, their fate will answer their call, and their night will then begin to fade, and their chains break and fall." A veteran dissident remarked, "He is leading us from the grave."[193]

In these representations, individuals spoke as if the outcome were determined, the civil side fated to win.

## Repressive Counter-Performances

No matter what its suggestive narrative power, the struggles that constituted the *mise en scène* did not have to end with victory for the revolutionary side. There really were twists and turns, and the Mubarak regime, even when it could not achieve a knockout punch, was often ahead on points. For three decades its rule had been successful in purely pragmatic terms, and its staying power was not effectuated by brute power alone. Mubarak tortured and killed some of his most determined opponents, but mostly he employed bribery, administrative control, and police power to co-opt his enemies and to prevent public performances of opposition. And he himself was always careful to keep up appearances, striving to appear as a strong and caring father for his citizen-children and hewing to his narrative that the regime was devoting itself, not only symbolically but materially, to bringing Egypt from the dark night of backwardness to the bright progressive light of the modern day. Machiavelli explained, "some men cherish something that seems like the real thing as much as they do the real thing itself."[194]

We have seen earlier that, far from presenting himself as the knife edge of naked power, Mubarak inserted his regime into the heart of moral classification, and he attacked the insurgency as a blocking character to his narrative of national progress and liberation. Throughout the eighteen days of twisting and turning, this conservative vision of purity and danger – this repressive sense of the narrative stake – informed every public speech-act of the regime. In "news" stories printed by state-controlled newspapers and in the "reports" of correspondents on state television and radio; in official statements by Mubarak's administrative staff; and in his own carefully crafted and widely broadcast speeches of 20 January and 10 February, Mubarak strove mightily to match his language of repression with the facts on the ground. "The government's strategy," the *New York Times* reported, "seems motivated at turning broader public opinion in the country against the protestors."[195] The dictator wished to connect emerging social facts to the right kind of signifiers, transforming them into signs that would speak in his chosen way. But the conjuring tricks of this master ventriloquist were losing their magical effect. Egypt's layered audiences seemed ever more distant from his megaphone. There was another powerful speaker in the national echo chamber, and the means of symbolic production were no longer Mubarak's to control. As journalists discovered to their surprise in the early days of the demonstrations, "Mubarak and his officials seemed to stumble in formulating a response to the most serious challenge to his rule."[196]

As Mubarak found it rhetorically more difficult to match his words with things, he exercised the levers of power to make things themselves seem different on the ground. On the fifth day of the confrontation, the regime removed the police presence from the streets of Egypt's major cities and let thousands of hardened criminals out of four prisons – to predictable effect.

> In a collapse of authority, the police withdrew from major cities on Saturday, giving rein to gangs that stole and burned cars, looted ships and ransacked a fashionable mall, where dismembered mannequins for conservative Islamic dress were strewn over broken glass and puddles of water. Thousands of inmates poured out of four prisons, including the country's most notorious, Abu Zaabal and Wadi Natroun.[197]

With social things being altered in this manner – with real rampaging and disorder in neighborhoods and streets – the regime hoped that its polluting moral assignations could now take hold. "Egypt challenges anarchy!" a government-owned newspaper hopefully shouted the next day. Some members of the national audience undoubtedly were convinced. "At first, the words were right," a driver named Abu Sayyid al-Sayyid confided to a reporter, referring to the early promises and performances of the demonstrations. Faced with the new social situation – the dangerous and newly unstable facts on the ground – al-Sayyid explained he had now changed his mind: "The protests were peaceful – freedom, jobs and all that. But then the looting came and the thugs and thieves with it. Someone has to step in before there's nothing left to step into." Nagi Ahmed, a schoolteacher in Cairo hoped the demonstrations would end soon: "I want to go back to work

*Figure 3*   Screenshot from Al Jazeera

... The money I have is almost gone."[198] Shenouda Badawi, a twenty-year-old Coptic Christian engineering student expressed concern: "My mother and my sister are terrified. We need calm. The message has been heard. Mubarak must stay in power as long as the opposition needs to form a new structure. Otherwise there will be chaos."[199]

On 31 January, Mubarak appeared on state television, "in a meeting with military chiefs in what was portrayed as business as usual."[200] Throughout that Sunday, state television broadcast calls from Egyptians who claimed to be 100 per cent loyal to the regime. "Behind you are eighty million people, saying yes to Mubarak!" one exclaimed.[201] Abdelaziz Ibrahim Fayed, a camel-owner and perfume-shop salesman at the pyramids stated, "One million don't need Mubarak, and 84 million don't want him to leave."[202] According to the New York Times, however, such full-throated support was among the "rarest of comments across Cairo."[203] The regime's effort to legitimate the discourse of repression – by actually making neighborhoods and streets dangerous – had failed. The movement's discourse of liberation proved resilient, its projection via alternative means of symbolic production effective and broad. An independent newspaper portrayed the new dangers on the ground this way: "A Conspiracy by Security to Support the Scenario of Chaos."[204] Rather than connecting the anti-regime demonstrators to the rising disorder, in fact, Cairo residents were much more likely to blame the regime itself. "We're worried about the chaos, sure," remarked a film director, Selma al-Tarzi, as she joined friends in Tahrir Square. "But everyone is aware the chaos is generated by the government. The revolution is not generating the chaos."[205]

Thomas Hobbes' warning about performative failure is three centuries old, but it still rings true. "That which taketh away the reputation of Sincerity," wrote the theorist of *Leviathan*,[206] "is the doing or saying of such things, as appear to be signes, that what they require other men to believe, is not believed by themselves." Once the Mubarak regime's signifying efforts were made to seem deeply hypocritical, its final layer of legitimacy peeled off like old house paint in the hot summer sun. The steel edge of the knife blade was all that was left. As it turned out, Mubarak could not make full use of the knife, which was ultimately in the hands of the Egyptian army, but he brandished his blade with flourish and employed it in a deeply menacing way.

From the first day of the 25 January Revolution, Mubarak had deployed force to prevent radical public performances, and he redoubled his efforts at physical repression as the insurrection expanded. Mubarak's police fired water cannons to disperse the massing of protestors; when they continued to surge forward, his forces fired rubber bullets; and, when nothing seemed to work, they used real bullets to shoot and kill. Activists were abducted from the streets for days and weeks, put into lock down, tortured, and sometimes murdered. Hundreds of protestors were shot, many of them mortally, in the streets. On 28 January, the fourth day of the protests, the leadership called for a "Day of Rage" for Friday, the holy day of the Islamic week. Intertwining the sacred and secular, hundreds of thousands of audience-participants marched towards Tahrir Square. Mubarak's forces responded

**Figure 4**   Screenshot from Facebook of the Friday of Rage Event page

with the most brutal crackdown of the eighteen-day revolt. The day began with a near total blackout of communications. "The Internet suddenly showed no sign of life," *La Repubblica* reported, and "a couple of hours later even mobile phones, local and international lines collapsed."[207] Soon after, Egypt's counterterrorism forces were deployed and the interior ministry warned of "decisive measures."[208] The day proceeded with brigades of riot police, black-shirted security police, and undercover forces in civilian dress battering protestors at mosques, bridges, and intersections, as part of a massive effort to prevent them from reaching Tahrir Square.[209]

After miles of peacefully marching, the demonstrators were confronted by a thousand armed police, along with five armored vehicles and two fire trucks. There ensued a fierce struggle over access to a bridge leading into the center. In what came to be known as "The Battle of Kasr el-Nil Bridge," protestors ripped bricks from the streets to throw at policemen and defended themselves with handmade shields; the armed security forces charged them with water cannon, tear gas, rubber bullets, and eventually live ammunition. Nine hundred people were hurt, 400 hospitalized with critical injuries. Observers described the streets as "covered with pools of blood."[210] The pitched battle ended in the early hours of the next morning, with the Mubarak forces in full retreat and tens of thousands of protestors in the square to stay. Mohammed ElBaradei called it the battle of "the people versus the thugs," adding, "this is the work of a barbaric regime that is doomed."[211] As it turned out, he was right.

## The Epiphanic Moment and Place

For the hundreds of thousands of demonstrators, and for many among their riveted audiences at home and abroad, the violent confrontation that extended from the afternoon of 28 January to early the next morning was a palpitating experience of fear and righteous rage, and their eventual victory was cathartic. The battle's denouement marked an epiphanic moment in the revolutionary narrative. It was a rupture that created a sense of liminality, a time out of time.[212] The routines of everyday temporality were shattered, the future brought into the present, and time opened up to the possibility of utopian change. Announcing a "new era," Mohammed ElBaradei declared "today we are proud of Egyptians. We have restored our rights, restored our freedom, and what we have begun cannot be reversed."[213] " It's our 'independence day,' a true independence," exalted Popi, an accountant from Suez.[214] Ahmed, an owner of a medical laboratory in Suez, proclaimed "the barrier of fear has fallen."[215] A hole had been punched in historical time, and the opening would not be closed until the revolutionary curtain fell. From now until Mubarak's capitulation on 11 February, participants and observers would speak of being inside a "moment."

> 28 January: This is truly a historical moment, one that undoubtedly will be seen in hindsight as the beginning of when Egyptians took their country back from corrupt, out-of-touch leaders who knew not the people they claimed to rule.[216]
>
> 29 January: A day of "fury and freedom" – a historic moment for an Egypt that has seen anger and fury aplenty.[217]
>
> 30 January: The revolt which changes the history of the Middle East.[218]
>
> The sweaty young men were fired by the euphoria of what they called a revolutionary moment.[219]
>
> No one seemed to be sure where the moment would lead. But everyone understood that it was, in fact, a moment.[220]
>
> A moment the most enthusiastic call revolutionary.[221]
>
> 31 January: Anti-Mubarak protest brings moment of truth for U.S.[222]
>
> 2 February: In the euphoria of the moment.[223]
>
> An historic moment, and it is teaching the Arab world everything.[224]
>
> 3 February: The Middle East watched breathlessly at a moment as compelling as any in the Arab world in a lifetime.[225]
>
> Many ... said they had experienced this day as a moment of

grace.[226]

4 February: "Our current revolutionary moment."[227]

5 February: "This is our moment, our time, Mubarak has to go. He will never know how we feel. We want to live, not to struggle."[228]

7 February: "No one seems willing to surrender a moment that feels imbued with the idealism of defiance."[229]

8 February: "One brief shining moment."[230]

11 February: "A moment of transformation."[231]

12 February: Egypt's Moment.[232]

As stunning a moment as the Arab world has witnessed.[233]

This moment out of time was concentrated and consecrated in an epiphanic place: Tahrir Square. In ordinary times, the square was "cacophonous and dirty, full of crazed motorists in dilapidated cars," the buildings were aged, and the place "carried a bit of menace."[234] After its consecration, Tahrir Square became a "parallel capital" that was "an idea as much as a place,"[235] "the center of the center of Cairo."[236] Inside the square, one Egyptian remarked, "my vision goes a lot farther than my eyes can see."[237] Already on the first day a demonstrator named Mohammed Saleh stated, "This is an historic day in Egypt's history, because we have started to say 'no'. I'll tell my children someday that I was standing here in Tahrir Square."[238] The *Guardian* wrote: "In Tahrir Square, in the centre of Cairo, on Tuesday night [25 January], Egypt refound and celebrated its diversity. The activists formed a minor part of the gathering, what was there was The People."[239] After the protestors survived the Battle of Kasr el-Nil Bridge, these historic feelings became more deeply weighted:

Tents housed artists, one of whom declared that Tahrir was the Revolution of Light. There was something fitting in the description, an idea of the ephemeral and fleeting. "God has cured my ailments here," said Ali Seif, 52, a photographer who has been here since the uprising began, and who said he had diabetes and heart problems. "That's what freedom feels like," said Ibrahim Hamid, standing next to him ... Mohamed Farouq stood at the entrance to the Kasr el-Nil Bridge, the passageway to Tahrir. "You feel like this is the society you want to live in," he said."[240]

"It's like a giant party, there is a strong feeling of happiness. For a week, I've barely slept because I participate in night patrols to secure the area. And yet I'm not tired, because one can breathe normally because the fear is gone," said Aza, a 38 year old Suez resident and manager of a maritime shipping company.[241]

Tahrir Square had become a living and breathing microcosm of a civil sphere, the idealized world of dignity, equality, and expanded solidarity for which the democratic activists fought. The following is a post from WAAKS (English):

Welcome to the Republic of Tahrir square, Cairo: In addition to Freedom of speach [sic] and Democracy for all, we have the following FREE services: hospital, daily newspaper, kitchen for hot meals, security, artists corner, singing and slogans club, poetry competitions, border control, signs exhibition and political brainstorming. (9 February 2011)

A broadcaster on Al Jazeera (English) commented that "the square has become a mini-utopia in central Cairo. Political opinions aired, gender and sectarian divisions nowhere to be found. People feed and clothe each other here."[242] Another story on Al Jazeera (English) reported that, while "it is hard to say how the protesters' civic engagement is viewed outside the Tahrir Square," conversations "in several residential neighbourhoods over the last week" praised "the communal atmosphere" in the square. "'There is no strife in the square between Christians and Muslims,' said an elderly man named Omar, sitting in a coffee shop in the capital's Agouza neighbourhood. 'This is how it used to be in all of Egypt'."[243] *Le Monde* also described Tahrir Square in an utopian manner:

> Despite concerns, the bad omens and the dead, the irreducible Tahrir Square cultivates a friendly atmosphere where, for the moment, political differences are silent in order to focus on the common goal: the leader's departure. Volunteers pick up trash, sweep the streets, distributing water and blankets. Improvised soccer matches happen at night to keep warm. Two teams were created: "Bread" and "Freedom." On Sunday, "Bread" won.[244]

For the *New York Times*, the square had become "the epicenter of the uprising and a platform, writ small, for the frustrations, ambitions and resurgent pride of a generation claiming the country's mantle."[245]

> In a sun-basked square, [the] sense of empowerment has radiated across the downtown, where volunteers passed out free wafers, tea and cake. Youths swept streets, organized security and checked identification at checkpoints in a show of popular mobilization ... "For the first time, people feel like they belong to this place," said Selma al-Tarzi, a 33-year old film director.[246]

> The streets of Cairo are famously unkempt; people scatter their trash in the streets. But in the square, a minimum ground for expectations was set and met ... Abdel Reheem ... was walking

with a garbage bag, systematically leaning over to collect the empty plastic cups, cigarette butts and dirty tissues left by the tide of protesters who came every day. "I am cleaning because this is my home," he said, adding that it was not until he went to Tahrir that he began to think of himself as a citizen. "I am Egyptian again, not marginalized, not without value or dignity," he said. "I feel like I have planted a tree. Now I need to look after it."[247]

"You see all these people, with no stealing, no girls being bothered, and no violence," said Omar Saleh. "He's trying to tell us that without me, without the regime, you will fall into anarchy, but we have all told him, 'No.'"[248]

In a country made miserable by the petty humiliations of authority, Egyptians were welcomed to the square with boisterous greetings. "Thank God for your safety," men organized as guards declared. "Welcome, heroes!" others cried. "Come on and join the square." Most poignantly, they simply chanted, "These are the Egyptian people."[249]

Everyone in the society is here.[250]

A graphic design on WAAKS (English) mixed the Western Superman icon with the newly luminous Egyptian image of democratic protesters overflowing Tahrir Square. Pulling open his white Oxford shirt and rep stripe tie, Superman reveals, not the traditional body-hugging blue shirt with big red "S," but a "liberated" Tahrir Square.

Four days after the first wave of repression had been rebuffed, on 2 and 3 February, the Mubarak regime engaged in one last violent spasmodic effort to route the assembled demonstrators and retake the square: 1.500 more people were injured and new deaths reported.[251] The government's invasion was again repulsed. This time around, however, there was no

**Figure 5**    Iconic Representation of Revolution: Superman Meets Tahrir Square

catharsis. The epiphanic moment had already arrived, and it already had a place.

> "This is the revolution in our country, the revolution in our minds. Mubarak can stay for days or weeks but he cannot change that. We cannot go back."[252]
>
> "'We're not afraid,'" said Ashraf Abdel Razeq, 37, who works as a carpenter and watches the tanks at night. "We want to clean our society, and we're not going to let the tanks stop us."[253]
>
> "Right now, it's all here, protecting Tahrir Square," said Hisham Kassem, a veteran activist and publisher, who kept a wary eye on barricades built with corrugated tin, wrecked cars and trucks, barrels, buckets filled with sand and metal railing torn from the

curb. "We keep it tonight, and tomorrow the whole country is going to come out."[254]

To interpret this final spasm of violence, Al Jazeera reached for the signifying language of the democratic protest movement. Casting the event as yet another episode of brutal state repression, the Arabic television station broadcast a passionate narrative about purity confronting evil, and it promised that the moment of revelation – the true identity of protagonists and antagonists – was imminent:

حقيقة البلطجية المتصدون للتظاهرات المصرية

على ظهور خيول و جمال جاؤو دخلو ميدان التحرير شاهرين الصياط و العصي و القضان و ترشح التقديرات أن عددهم يفوت 3000. فمن يكون هؤلاء الذين فاجؤو الجميع بهجومهم... و الذين قالوا إنهم إعتقلوا بعض المهاجمين و عثروا معهم على بطاقات تثبت أنهم من رجال الشرطة. فقد ذكرت حركة السادس من أبريل أن المهاجمين هم رجال لشرطة بلباس مدني و بلطجية مأجورون من رجال أعمال. و قال محمد البردعي إن لديه أدلة على أن المهاجمين من الشرطة أما مصطفا الفقي من الحزب الحاكم فقال أنه من مأجوري بعض رجال الأعمال من الحزب الحاكم...مطالبات سلمية للشباب تقمع بالحديد و النار و الأسلحة الميلة للدموع و حصيلة القتلى و سئات من الجرحى. والداخلية تنفي – و الجيش على الحياد و يبقى الجواب عن هوية القامعين أو المجرمين حسب المنظمات الحقوقية في طي الأيام المقبلة و في أحكام القضاء.

**Thugs Confront Egyptian Protestors**

On the backs of horses and camels they came, entering into Tahrir Square, brandishing whips, crowbars, and other weapons, their numbers running to an estimated 3000. So who are those that came attacking ... Protesters say that they have captured some of the attackers and find on them cards certifying that they are policemen. The April 6 Movement claimed that the attackers are plain-clothes policemen and thugs hired by businessmen. Mohamed ElBaradei said that he had evidence that the attackers were from among the police. Mustafa AlFaqi from the ruling party said that some are on the payroll of businessmen from the ruling party ... The demands of peaceful young people are suppressed with iron and fire, with tear gas, resulting in many killed and hundreds wounded. And the Interior ministry denies it all – the army remains neutral and the answer ... as to the identity of criminals and oppressors ... will be left up to judgment of the next few days.[255]

## The Sense of an Ending

With the symbolic center firmly secured, the victory of the revolution became only a matter of time. Mubarak made one more effort to alter the facts on the ground, trying once again to match the regime's words with things. At the beginning of week three, the government staged another performance of "normalization." The revolutionary occupation of Tahrir Square was now taken as a fait accompli, so rather than engage in a futile effort at polluting it, the government tried making it seem mundane. Before 25 January, Cairo's overflowing cars had passed with difficulty through the square's traffic-jammed streets; after that date, passage was blocked by the confluence of revolutionaries, barbed wire, homemade barricades, army trucks and tanks. The regime now proposed to restore traffic by routing it around the square rather than through it. Banks were scheduled to be reopened, newspapers taken down from shop windows, and Egypt's stock market was to start doing business for the first time in days.[256] With these practical alterations underway, the regime tried reconnecting its social signifiers with social facts. Officials declared the revolt a thing of the past, and two days later Mubarak gave a rambling and paternalistic speech. Wheeling out its tired and hoary platitudes, the regime polluted the revolutionaries by working the binaries one last time. Framing the massive civil disobedience as "extremely dangerous," the recently appointed vice-president Omar Suleiman claimed continued revolt would lead to "uncalculated and hasty steps that produce more irrationality." To prevent such degradation, the insurrection must be shut down and the regime allowed to thrive. "There will be no ending of the regime," Suleiman declared, "because that means chaos," and "we absolutely do not tolerate it."[257] But the voice and the actions of the dictatorship no longer had performative traction. The failure of Mubarak's earlier fact-altering efforts had first compelled him to unsheathe the cold edge of the knife blade. If that earlier violence had proven unable to shut down the revolutionary performance, how could the regime now declare normality and just move on?

One performance on 7 February did succeed in garnering sympathetic public attention. It was the fairy-tale of Wael

Ghonim's release. Twelve days earlier, the Facebook organizer had been kidnapped, secreted in a government location, imprisoned and kept in blindfolded isolation. His last tweet before his disappearance had ominously evoked martyrdom: "Pray for #Egypt. Very worried as it seems that government planning a war crime against people. We are all ready to die #Jan25."[258] His first tweet after liberation evoked the sacrality of the civil struggle: "Freedom is a bless that deserves fighting for it [sic]." The evening of his release, Ghonim appeared on Egypt's most popular interview show, *10 P.M.*, broadcast by satellite television. Resolving a long-standing mystery, he identified himself as the creator of "We Are All Khalid Said." The Facebook page that helped build and direct the participant-audience of the revolution now had 486,000 registered followers.[259] As the tearful and handsome young man recounted his suffering and resurrection, he gestured to the revolutionary narrative and the protagonists who had died for it.

> "Please do not make me a hero," Mr. Ghonim said in a voice trembling with emotion, and later completely breaking down when told of the hundreds of people who have died in clashes since the Jan. 25 protests began. "I want to express my condolences for all the Egyptians who died. We were down there for peaceful demonstrations," he added. "The heroes were the ones on the street."[260]

The interview helped transform Ghonim into what one observer called the "movement's reluctant icon." The next day, he and the talk show host Mona el-Shazly, a star in her own right, made a pilgrimage to Tahrir Square. When demonstrators converged in greater numbers than ever before, Ghonim and el-Shazly "were the ones many came to cheer."[261]

Two days after that, on 10 February, with worker strikes outside Cairo adding to the momentum and giant demonstrations continuing in the square, Mubarak scheduled a nationally televised address, and leaks from inside and outside Egypt created sky-high expectations he would resign. But the president tried once more to match his authoritarian version of the progressive narrative with the new facts on the Egyptian ground. Assuring demonstrators "your demands are ... legitimate and just," he praised them "for being a symbolic generation that is calling for change to the better, that is dreaming for a better future, and is making the future." Refusing to budge, he placed his historical persona on the side of the future: "I'm determined to execute and carry out what I have promised without going back to the past."[262] The hundreds of thousands in Tahrir Square fairly bellowed in frustration and rage, shaking their shoes at his televised image. Earlier that day, the Supreme Council of the Armed Forces had issued a document entitled "Communique Number 1," on behalf of which, on state television, an army spokesman affirmed "support for the legitimate demands of the people" and pledged to "remain in continuous session to consider what procedures and measures ... may be taken to protect the nation, and the achievements and aspirations of the great people of Egypt."[263] Afterward, the army chief of staff came to Tahrir Square and made similar assurances, and the crowd roared in celebration. The steel edge of the knife blade was sheathed. Not coercive but civil power would determine the outcome of this historic confrontation.

Hosni Mubarak resigned early the next evening. Under the heading "Collective Effervescence," the *New York Times* wrote how "tens of thousands who had bowed down for evening prayers leapt to their feet, bouncing and dancing in joy," that "revising the sense of the revolution's rallying cry, they chanted, 'the people, at last have brought down the regime'."[264] The courageous protagonists had won, and the inverted arc of national history would rise again. An Egyptian told the *Wall Street Journal*:

> Gamal Abdul Nasser and Anwar Al Sadat and Hosni Mubarak had taken away from me the love of my country ... I despaired of our people, thought they had given up liberty for this mediocre tyranny. Then on January 28, leaving the Friday prayer, I saw an endless stream of humanity, heading to Liberation Square. I never thought I would live to see this moment, these people in that vast crowd, they gave me back my love of my country.[265]

The epiphanic character of the revolution was celebrated and its sacrality affirmed. Writing for the *Guardian*, the novelist Ahdaf Soueif observed: "The joy cries filled the air – across Egypt the joy cries filled the air ... Look at the streets of Egypt; this is what hope looks like."[266] A protestor exalted, "the sun will rise on a more beautiful Egypt."[267] "I'm in Tahrir Square!" a young man yelled into his cell phone, spreading the word, "in freedom, in freedom, in freedom."[268] The *Wall Street Journal* ran these captions beneath photographs portraying the regime's denouement.[269]

> People celebrating in Alexandria waved signs, hung out car windows, and danced on the sea wall.

A man kneeled in a road and prayed in Alexandria.

Many families joined in the celebration in Alexandria.

People celebrating in Tahrir Square in Cairo used aerosol cans to create streaks of fire.

A man gazed towards a screen in Tahrir Square.

A man in Cairo held up a laptop displaying an image of celebrations in Egypt after hearing the news that Mr. Mubarak was resigning.

Two men embraced in Tahrir Square after hearing that Mr. Mubarak was resigning.

People lighted flares in Tahrir Square.

Flares illuminated the crowd in Tahrir Square.

The sense of an out-of-time moment could not be contained. An Egyptian announcer on the Hezbollah-run television in Al-Manar wept on air. "Allahu Akbar, the pharaoh is dead," he announced, asking "Am I dreaming? I'm afraid to be dreaming."[270] Wael Ghonim had marked the first day of revolution by tapping to his WAAKS followers his "feeling that I'm in a dream." When the revolutionary performance succeeded, Ghonim insisted to his fellow Egyptians that dreaming was a civil obligation: "It shows how civilized the Egyptian people are. Now our nightmare is over. It's time to dream."[271]

## Of Power Physical, Interpretive, and Global

Meanings make revolutions. But the collective and individual actors who crystallize and perform revolutionary meanings do not do so in circumstances of their own choosing. Only rarely do they possess the communicative means to project their interpretations effectively, much less the physical means to protect their performances from violence by the powers that be.

## The Means of Symbolic Production

Effective social performances rely on powerful background representations, skillful directors who can write and direct scripts, motivated and convincing actors, and a twisting and turning *mise en scène* to build the suspense that makes an audience rapt. None of this matters, however, if a performance does not have access to the means of symbolic production. In the first place, performers must have a stage. But even with a stage – like the streets and squares of Cairo – social performance needs access to the media of mass communication. Without distributive power, the revolution cannot have interpretive power: it cannot project to audiences who remain at one remove from the immediate face-to-face.

On the evening of 28 January, during the ferocious struggles between demonstrators and armed civilians and police, state television broadcast a "quiet tableau of the night sky in downtown Cairo, with the message that a curfew had been imposed."[272] That morning the government had tried pulling the plug on Egypt's internet connection to remove the nation from the global grid. Yet, despite these efforts, Al Jazeera television managed to run live video of the raging battle right up to the victory of demonstrators early in the morning of 29 January.

In the midst of the battle, on its Arabic channel's program

"Egypt's Revolution," Al-Jazeera journalist Fawzi al-Bushra delivered his report alongside dramatic televised scenes of tear gas being fired; plain-clothes police officers beating a young man; massed demonstrators fighting against a tear-gas-firing armored vehicle and then being run down by it; individual protestors being shot; and old men and women, with emotionally stricken faces and voices, demanding Mubarak's ouster. Al-Bushra's takeaway from the ugly confrontations was the golden rule of civil society. "After many dead, wounded, and arrested numbering in the thousands," he observed, "the people discovered ... that the police aren't always in the service of the people and can sometimes resort to oppression when the people don't line up with the will of the rulers." Because "the government became estranged from its people, secluded, and incapable," it had "kept quiet about the events," but now they were being "broadcast to television screens around the world."[273]

At one point, Al Jazeera's Arabic and English channels both displayed a split screen that juxtaposed the peaceful scene broadcast by state television with pictures of a police van set on fire by protestors defying the curfew, amid sounds of gunfire and explosions.[274] These sounds and images of state repression and courageous resistance were beamed up from Tahrir Square to satellites circulating the earth, distributed to sympathetic Arab audiences outside Cairo, flashed across the entire globe, and broadcast back to some protesters inside.

The omnipresence of such alternative images and texts would have been unthinkable two decades earlier, when the capacity for dictatorships to censor broadcasts was virtually airtight.[275] In 1989, the Chinese army carried out deadly killings of Tiananmen protestors under conditions of a blackout so total that documentary evidence of the repression is not available to this day. Contemporary digital technology has destroyed such governmental capacity to monopolize the means of broadcast communication.[276] It has facilitated the rise of alternative media, whether commercial entertainment television, private or independent news journalism, or web-based media such as blogs and social media. During the 25 January Revolution, each of these digital-based technologies, at one time or another and in varying degrees of intensity, played a critical role in allowing radical political performances to project themselves beyond their immediate staging, reaching potentially sympathetic audiences on the outside. The operational capacity for none of these alternative media was based entirely inside Egyptian territory. They all employed satellites, so one source of their distributive machinery circled the globe beyond national control. Yet, each of these media also depended on ground receivers, on downloadable and uploadable capacities, either cell-phone or computer-based. Attacking these on-the-ground elements of digital technologies, the Egyptian state traded its immediate economic interest – much of its wealth also depended on digital communication – for a shot at destroying its opponent's ability to wage an effective symbolic fight.

The response to these efforts at controlling the means of symbolic production demonstrates how the anti-authoritarian capacity of digital media depends, not only on technological ingenuity, but on democratic commitment. It was the moral outrage of technicians, managers, and owners, as much as their technical abilities, that was required to combat the repressive effects of government might:

> A senior strategist at National Public Radio, whose day job was in digital media, turned his personal Twitter account into a news wire. Seeking out voices and videos inside Egypt, he made 400 new posts a day to some 20,800 followers, many of whom were professional journalists with access to new media from around the world.[277]

> After the Egyptian state shut down uploading to Twitter, activists inside Twitter and Google developed a news service, Speak2tweet, that allowed Egyptians without access to digital media to leave cell phone voice messages that could be filed as updates to Twitter.[278]

> After the Internet went back up, managers at YouTube working with Storyful, a social media curatorial service, discovered a way to retrieve and store the thousands of videos pouring out of Tahrir Square and to make them quickly accessible on CitizenTube, its news and politics channel.[279]

Each of the above items represents an ingenious technological achievement, but each also depended on its enablers having a will, not only a way. The owners of digital media could have cooperated with the Egyptian government and shut down their media without a fight. Egyptian performances of democracy influenced them to behave in exactly the opposite way.

> "Like many people, we've been glued to the news unfolding in Egypt and thinking of what we could do to help people on the ground," said a joint statement posted Monday by Ujjwal Singh, the co-founder of SayNow, and Abdel Karim Mardini, Google's

product manager for the Middle East and North Africa. "Over the weekend we came up with the idea of a speak-to-tweet device – the ability for anyone to tweet using just a voice connection," the statement said. "We hope that this will go some way to helping people in Egypt stay connected at this very difficult time. Our thoughts are with everyone there."[280]

## The Global Civil Sphere

It is notable that such supportive comments came from controllers of media technology located outside of Egypt. That the revolutionary performance inside Egypt unfolded not only before local but international audiences was a critical reason, not only for its ultimate success, but for its very ability to proceed. In the middle of the worst days of government repression, an Egyptian novelist confided to a Western journalist that, "even if the regime continues to bombard us with bullets and tear gas, and continues to block Internet access and cutoff our mobile phones, we will find ways to get our voices across the world and to demand freedom and justice."[281] He was confident the brutal physical power of the Egyptian regime could be restrained if protestors connected to the broader civil sphere outside. He was correct that, in the age of digital media, he and his colleagues could find ways to continue to project their civil productions beyond the national territory. He was also right that there would be a massive world audience to respond to demands for freedom and justice.[282] Yet, the global audience is fragmented, the perception of geopolitical interest matters as much as civil ideals, and the invocation of both global public opinion and sanctions is skewed in hegemonic, north-versus-south, west-versus-east kinds of ways.[283]

The United States and other capitalist democracies compromise their internal commitments to civil society in order to protect what they conceive as geopolitical interests, and in the Egyptian case there seemed to be many such interests indeed, from supporting Israel to fighting Islamic terrorism to maintaining stable oil production and prices. Some of these national interests are material, having to do with matters of life and limb and economic concerns of the gravest kind; others are moral, having to do with protecting a Jewish state in the post-Holocaust world. Whether material or ideal, during the days of the 25 January Revolution such interests formed an external environment in relation to which the American nation-state felt compelled to act in an instrumentally rational way. Regardless of commitments in principle to a civil society, national leaders felt the United States' interests would be damaged by a revolutionary upheaval. At first, they opposed the democratic movement and supported Mubarak's continuing reign. After the first day of demonstrations in Egypt, US Secretary of State Hillary Clinton, even while protesting, "we support the fundamental right of expression and assembly for all people," and while urging "all parties" to "exercise restraint and refrain from violence," offered an extraordinarily realpolitik "assessment" of the situation: "The Egyptian Government is stable and is looking for ways to respond to the legitimate needs and interests of the Egyptian people."[284] Nor did other democratic states offer Egyptian insurgents immediate support.

On the global level, despite Japan's democratic capitalism

and China's rise, the global exercise of economic and military power remains largely limited to a handful of Western states, states which have chosen to bind their internal exercise of political power in a democratic way.[285] In Britain, France, and the United States, the civil sphere exercises ultimate control over the state. Civil power manifests itself in public opinion, which is powerfully affected by independent journalism. In the earliest days of Egypt's 25 January Revolution, Western media coverage was torn between two metaphors. In the poetics that sought to make sense of this titanic struggle, one finds the stark metaphorical contrast between 1979 and 1989.[286] "If Egyptian protesters overcome the government," the *New York Times* asked, "would this be 1979 or 1989?"[287] Which historical memory should be analogically applied? Were the events in 2011 Egypt like the anti-communist revolutions in Europe of 1989? Or did they resemble 1979 Iran, when the overthrow of the Shah, which at first seemed democratic, quickly gave way to a violent and repressive theocratic dictatorship? In 2011, a *New York Times* editorial warned "the Iranian Revolution is seared in our memories,"[288] one of its columnists recalling how "in 1979, a grass-roots uprising in Iran led to an undemocratic regime that oppresses women and minorities and destabilizes the region."[289] Perhaps, however, Egyptians were experiencing a revolution like the one in 1989? As the *New York Times* reminds its readers, "in 1989, uprisings in Eastern Europe led to the rise of stable democracies."[290] If the 1979 metaphor applied, then the contentious events in Egypt would be signified as wild, out of control, and sinister. If, however, Egyptians were actually inside a "1989" revolution, then events in 2011, while still contentious and often chaotic, could be coded as civil, and eminently worthy of identification and respect.

As the revolutionary performance inside Egypt became more powerful and sharply etched, the metaphorical confusion waned. The insurgency was less ambiguously framed. It became the "Arab Spring," and the 1989 metaphor applied. One *Le Monde* report put it this way:

> We're not in 1979. The Islamic revolution was a great disappointment. Young Arabs connected to the Internet have seen the videos of these young Iranians killed by the henchmen of Ahmadinejad. They identify more with them, or young Tunisians than with the "beards." In the streets, the few "Allah Akbar" are drowned out by cries of "freedom."[291]

Another *Le Monde* report was even more generous, linking the events in Egypt with the nation's own sacred date of 1789, the year of the French Revolution.[292] *La Repubblica* also became less ambivalent:

> Egyptian civil society has been growing and restructuring. Certainly, there is the Muslim Brotherhood, an archipelago of a thousand ambiguities, which Mubarak has sold successfully as a band of terrorists. But there are also non-Christians, nationalists, socialists, people who can no longer simply tolerate the "hereditary republic". The less we listen and support their demands, the more the risk of an Islamist drift becomes concrete.[293]

This metaphorical shift was not limited to the left. Conservative media also began to manifest enthusiasm for the civil, revolutionary side.[294] An editorial in *USA Today* announced that "Egypt is not post-Shah Iran"[295] and another concluded that "a foreign policy that stands in opposition to American ideals – in Egypt as elsewhere – is one that is doomed to failure."[296]

Indeed, the enthusiasm of Western media for the Egyptian revolution has been on display throughout the pages of this essay, evidenced in the hundreds of citations to influential media in France, Italy, the UK, and the US, and to the broadcasts beamed into these domestic civil spheres from Al Jazeera (English). While the reports from these professional journalists were detached, they were not "objective" but interpretive judgments. Journalists evaluated the revolution's unfolding events in relation to the overarching discourse of civil society, a standard that reflected not only the professional ethics of journalists but the commitments of democratic constituencies back home. In turn, such reporting affected opinion in the civil spheres of Western nations.[297] Al Jazeera's Arabic reporting powerfully influenced Egypt's emerging civil sphere in a similar way. Presenting themselves as both professionally independent and deeply democratic, Al Jazeera journalists deployed the moral binaries of civil discourse to sentimentalize the revolution's protagonists and stigmatize its enemies.[298] Between such Arabic and Western journalism there was, in fact, a marked intertextuality, with each side referring frequently to the other's reporting to make its own points. In a broadcast early on 25 January, for example, Al Jazeera (Arabic) reported that "an American reporter in Cairo for *Time* magazine described the protests that are expected to take place today [as] similar to the popular outpouring that caused the fall of Zine El Abidine Ben Ali in Tunis" and as an "historical event with respect to popular political activity in the age of Hosni Mubarak."[299] The broadcast ended with this news:

وقد حثت منظمة العفو الدولية السلطات المصرية على "السماح بالاحتجاجات السلمية"، وقال متعاطفون من مختلف أنحاء العالم إنهم يعتزمون تنظيم احتجاجات للتضامن مع الاحتجاجات في مصر.

And Amnesty International urged the Egyptian authorities to "allow peaceful protests," and sympathizers from around the world said that they intend to organize protests in solidarity with protests in Egypt.[300]

Western journalists, for their part, often referred to Arabic reports in Al Jazeera to provide evidence of the depth and breadth of the democratic uprising among the Egyptian people.

No wonder that Egyptian state authorities threatened, intimidated, and often physically attacked journalists throughout the revolutionary fight. Such incidents often had a boomerang effect, however, transforming journalists from implicit into explicit protagonists in the dramatic struggle between liberty and repression, a transformation that supplied "global civil society" with new heroes in its critical reaction to the Egyptian state. In the UK, the *Guardian* provided a detailed first-hand account of correspondent Jack Shenker's physical assault and arrest by security forces alongside Egyptian protestors.[301] Al-Jazeera and CNN broadcast similar stories about attacks on their leading correspondents.[302]

## The Army

Social performances are always mediated by power, and not only of the interpretive kind. That the Egyptian army refrained from exercising its physical power is what allowed the agonistic performances of government and protestors to play out, for the revolutionary confrontation to be in greater part symbolic, and for the radicals to make such an arresting case that civil power compelled Mubarak to leave the scene.

In democracies, the civil sphere places extraordinary physical, administrative, legal, and cultural constraints upon the exercise of massed violence inside the territory of the nation-state. A nation's armed forces have the physical power many times over to control domestic disputes, but even in civil emergencies, when the internal activation of military force is authorized, officers of the civil sphere issue orders that greatly inhibit physical fire power. Because authoritarian societies do not possess such civil constraints, the armed forces frequently exercise, and even more frequently threaten to exercise, massive physical power on the domestic scene. Certainly, this was the case in post-colonial Egypt, where presidents Nasser, Sadat, and Mubarak all rose from the ranks of the army and made use of its physical capacities for all sorts of domestic tasks.

Why the army failed to intervene during the 25 January Revolution has often been explained by material interest. That the army wished to preserve its wealth and status is certainly not to be denied. If these were its primary motives, however, military leaders would have sided with autocracy, for Mubarak fed, clothed, and pampered them, and wished them always at his side. But perhaps the army refrained from repression from fear they would be injured by the backlash from democratic public opinion? This might indeed have happened, but why would the army have cared, if they lived in a privileged and isolated manner, had the physical power to protect themselves, and if only its material self-interest was at stake?

In fact, there is evidence that many of the army's highest officers, as well as its mass of draftees, were attracted to the emotions and ideals projected by revolutionary performances. Many of the staff were trained by, and spent long periods of time in, Western democratic countries, particularly the United States, where contentious democratic conflicts are rife and civil inhibitions still rule. For the first time in decades, Mubarak did order army troops actively to intervene in Egypt's political life, yet the army, while agreeing to be present, chose to remain aloof. Not the army, but Mubarak's secret police and specially recruited civilians were the forces that violently intervened. In the epiphanic moment that followed the 28 January battle between revolutionaries trying to enter Tahrir Square and police forces blocking it, the army declared its respect for the civil cause of the protestors and refused to physically intervene:

> The six day uprising here entered a new stage about 9 p.m. when a uniformed spokesman declared on state television that "the armed forces will not resort to the use of force against our great people" ... The military understood "the legitimacy of your demands" and "affirms that freedom of expression through peaceful means is guaranteed to everybody."[303]

By the evening of 29 January, the side that the army was taking had become manifest and clear.

> On the 6th October bridge, as darkness fell, a couple of dozen police were attempting to hold their positions confronted by a crowd of several thousands. It was under this bridge that the Guardian saw the first army vehicles, two armoured infantry carriers, motoring down the Nile Corniche, news of their arrival cheered by demonstrators. By 7.45pm a column of army tanks was visible, rumbling across the Abd El Moniem Riyad overpass, flying Egyptian flags. Some of them had protesters dancing on them as they drove along.[304]

For their part, throughout the demonstrations, protestors expressed solidarity with the army:

> Egyptian protesters in Cairo chanted slogans calling for the army to support them, complaining of police violence during clashes on Friday in which security forces fired teargas and rubber bullets. "Where is the army? Come and see what the police are doing to us. We want the army."[305]

> Adel, an engineer conscripted into the army, had shed his military uniform and joined the protesters, watching as the tanks rolled across the street. He warned that deaths were inevitable. "Some soldiers won't fire on the Egyptian people, but others are too scared to disobey orders. You have no idea what rebelling in the army can mean for you." He continued: "I am supposed to be on the 7am train to my barracks, but we are witnessing the final hours of Mubarak and his regime."[306]

> ElBaradei, who is now backed by the powerful Muslim Brotherhood and other opposition groups, said he wanted to negotiate about a new government with the army, which he described as "part of the Egyptian people."[307]

> Tanks surround Tahrir Square but the army has declared it will never attack the people. Young Egyptians surround the tanks, chatting with the soldiers. Last night there was a football game – "the people versus the army" – with a tank as the prize. The people won. They did not get the tank. But then one of the most popular chants in Tahrir today is: "The people, the army as one hand."[308]

> Mostafa Hussein, a rights activist, said: "I have to admit I feel anxious about the future. I worry the military will try to control the country with an iron fist. The only thing I can be certain of is that they won't open fire and try to kill us en masse."[309]

> Tawfik El-Mardenly ... 62, managing director of a telecom company, served as a private before the 1973 war against Israel. "We never say anything bad about the army," he said. "They gave us the only victory in our life," he said, referring to 1973 war that led to strategic gains for Egypt. "People don't see them as corrupt, unlike the police." He added, "We respect the army, and we would like to keep this respect as long as we can. This is not the army's role."[310]

It was when the army publicly reaffirmed its commitment to the civil cause, on the penultimate day of the confrontation, that Egypt's dictator had no practical option but to resign.

The argument for material interest can also be externally made. The reason for the army's exercise of self-constraint may be seen as responding to threats from hegemonic powers, if not from global civil society. It is a fact that nation-states and their armies monopolize the means of violence on the global scene. In a global order more Hobbesian that Lockean, hegemonic control operates at both regional and international levels. With many times the national military budget of other nations, significant technological advantages, a vast military network of alliances, and robust if often precarious international prestige, the US government often uses threats of military intervention, and sometimes the real thing, to gain international control. While it did not threaten to directly intervene in Egypt, the American military still had significant effect. Early on, Vice-President Joe Biden publically warned the Egyptian army that, if it did intervene against the protestors, the United States would "review its commitments" to supplying its annual $1.3 billion military aid. From that point on, American military officers at every level made frequent informal contacts with their Egyptian counterparts, warning them against intervention.[311]

This exercise of American power over the Egyptian army was significant. It begs the question, however, of why the United States should wish to prevent the army's physical intervention in the first place. Answering this question takes the search for an explanation from the material back to the ideal side. The democratic reporting of journalists affected domestic public opinion, which then exerted civil power against government support for Mubarak. Reporters' sympathetic interpretations, outraged letters to editors,[312] influential op-ed columnists, and the deeply bred civil distaste for anti-democratic oppression had a cumulative effect. "Faced with images of riot police using tear gas and water cannons," the *New York Times* reported, "President Obama moved from support to distancing."[313] Before long, the world's most powerful democratic nations were engaged in speech acts strongly sanctioning Mubarak and supporting the revolutionary movement. President

Barack Obama and Secretary of State Hillary Clinton continually warned Egyptian officials to "allow peaceful public demonstrations" and reminded them that people needed "mechanisms to express legitimate grievances." When the plug was pulled on the internet, US officials immediately issued blunt criticisms. As the revolutionary process travelled farther down the road, Secretary Clinton began repeating, "We have been very clear that we want to see an orderly transition to democracy,"[314] and key European leaders also publicly urged "restraint."[315] By the second week of the insurrection, as Mubarak became increasingly polluted by the protest, the *New York Times* reported that "Obama seemed determined to put as much daylight as possible" between himself and the Egyptian president.[316] Government sources leaked the story that, months before the January crisis, the American president had ordered an intensive secret policy review of the US Egyptian policy, which resulted in a classified eighteen-page "Presidential Study Directive," and that, during the crisis, Obama had devoted thirty-eight meetings to the topic.[317] In a televised speech to the American people hours after Mubarak's resignation, Obama projected deep sympathy for the civil struggle of the Egyptian revolution. "Egyptians have made it clear that nothing less than genuine democracy will carry the day," he declared. Evoking the iconic language of Martin Luther King, Obama connected the Egyptian struggle to the most revered movement of civil repair in America's own recent history. In Egypt, he declared, "it was the moral force of nonviolence − not terrorism and mindless killing − that bent the arc of history toward justice once more."[318]

Because public opinion in Western democratic societies mattered, Egyptian protestors directed messages to the communicative institutions of the global civil sphere. Explaining why English was the major language other than Arabic in which the Tahrir Square protestors inscribed their signs, an academic said it was "to assert the country is modern and its citizens know the global language" and to combat "Western stereotypes about being backward and traditional."[319] In part because of the United States' hegemonic power, but also because of Obama's race and family background and the way he had reached out to Islamic civilization with his earlier "Cairo speech," the American president often received from the Egyptian protesters disproportionate attention:

> Many of the protesters were critical of the United States and complained about American government support for Mr. Mubarak [but] many of the protesters expressed their criticisms by telling American journalists that they had something to tell the president, directly. "I want to send a message to President Obama," said Mohamed el-Mesry, a middle-aged professional. "I call on President Obama, at least in his statements, to be in solidarity with the Egyptian people and freedom, truly like he says."[320]

WAAKS (English) projected a continuous stream of text, image, and sound from inside the heart of the revolution to English reading and listening audiences in the wider world around. After the first day of confrontations, on 25 January, the Facebook page sent out this message:

> Good night everyone. A kind request to our international supporters: Make your voice heard, tell your representatives

and members of parliament that you do not wish for your government to support dictatorships like Mubarak's. (26 January 2011, 1.56 a.m.)

Early on 28 January, the day of massive confrontation, WAAKS (English) posted:

It really feels like World population is becoming one nation. The amount of support we are getting from brave international individuals and groups is enormous. Wikileaks has just published fresh cables about Egyptian police brutality. Nothing new to us, but let the world see. I'll be posting a lot of news very soon. get ready. (28 January 2011, 12.49 p.m.)

Some hours later, this post:

Many many thanks for the international solidarity. Individuals from all over the world have proved to themselves & to all of us that we are just ONE human race despite any differences. Please watch this excellent video by our supporters: A Guerilla Projection and "Remove Mubarak" on the UN building in New York. (28 January 2011, 7.43 p.m.)

Finally, toward the end of the 28 January battle:

Please everyone. Don't let Egyptians suffer alone. Your support and pressure does make a lot of difference. Protest peacefully in your country, lobby your leaders & government, if the world turns on Mubarak, he will have to leave under pressure. (29 January 2011, 1.53 a.m.)

On 11 February, WAAKS (English) posted this revolutionary denouement:

THANK GOD. THANKS TO ALL THOSE WHO DIED FOR US TO LIVE IN FREEDOM. THANKS TO ALL EGYPTIANS WHO SLEPT

ROUGH IN TAHRIR, ALEXANDRIA AND EVERYWHERE. THANK
YOU ALL ON THIS PAGE FOR YOUR SUPPORT AND YOUR
AMAZING GREATNESS AND HELP. THANKS TO EVERYONE
WHO CALLED HIS LEADER AND HIS REPRESENTATIVE. THANK
YOU TUNISIA. (11 February 2011, 6.54 p.m.)

* * *

The 25 January movement needed not only highly charged
background representations, a dedicated carrier group, an
effective script, skillful performances, a twisting and turning
plot, digital technology, a wired population, sympathetic
Western civil spheres, courage, and *fortuna*. It also required
a special relationship between the United States and the
Egyptian army to make its cultural revolution come out right.

Whether it will stay right is too early to say. The same army
that stepped aside so the civil drama could unfold now – at
the time of this writing – exercises unchallengeable control.
This irony has been lost neither on the revolutionary carrier
group nor the masses of Egyptians who joined them. During
the interim period, the army kept a tight lid, not only on the old
regime, but on performances of democracy itself. Nonetheless,
Egypt's constitution has been amended to limit terms in high
office, the leaders of Mubarak's government have been jailed,
the old ruling party disbanded, and parliamentary elections
presently scheduled for November 2011.

There has been an extraordinary cultural upheaval in
Egyptian society, and its symbolic effects will reverberate for
years and decades to come. Two months after the political
curtain of the revolution came down, an Egyptian court ordered

the erasure of the names and images of Hosni Mubarak and his wife "from all squares, streets, schools, associations, libraries and all entities in Egypt."[321] Judge Muhammad Hassan Omar explained that their continued presence caused "tremendous harm and continuous suffering" to the families of those who had died during the weeks of protest. Not only Mubarak, but the ideals he represented, remain deeply polluted. To complete the process of purification, Egyptians will have to continue moving forward in a democratic way.

# Notes

1 Fawzi al-Bushra, "Egyptian Revolution," Al Jazeera (Arabic), 28 January 2011, http://www.youtube.com/watch?v=JYuxjgU6yeE&feature=channel_video_title [accessed 10 June 2011].

2 Souad Mekhennet and Nicholas Kulish, "With Muslim Brotherhood Set to Join Egypt Protests, Religion's Role May Grow," *New York Times*, 28 January 2011, A10.

3 Charles M. Blow, "The Kindling of Change," *New York Times*, 5 February 2011, A17.

4 Cécile Hennion, "Un Mouvement de Contestation Gagne l'Egypte," *Le Monde*, 27 January 2011, 5.

5 "Egypt: Rage Against the Mubaraks," *Guardian*, 27 January 2011, 36. See also Charles Levinson and Sam Dagher, "Rallies Fan Out as Regime Closes Ranks," *Wall Street Journal* (online), 9 February 2011, http://online.wsj.com/article/SB1000142405274870485840457613 3630107794342.html [accessed 20 June 2011].

6 Paul Mason, "Twenty Reasons Why It's Kicking Off Everywhere," 'Idle Scrawl Blog', BBC (online), 5 February 2011, http://www.bbc.co.uk/blogs/newsnight/paulmason/2011/02/twenty_reasons_why_its_kicking.html [accessed 10 June 2011].

7 Michael Slackman, "In Mideast Activism, a New Tilt Away from Ideology," *New York Times*, 23 January 2011, 10.

8 Mona El-Naggar and Michael Slackman, "Egypt's Leader Used Old Tricks to Defy New Demands," *New York Times*, 28 January 2011, A11.

9 Simon Sebag Montefiore, "Every Revolution Is Revolutionary in Its Own Way," *New York Times*, 27 March 2011, "Review" 11.

10 Emmanuel Todd, "Interview by Lara Ricci," *Il Sole 24 Ore* (online), 26 February 2011, http://lararicci.blog.ilsole24ore.com [accessed 12 June 2011]. These remarks referenced the interviewee's earlier

work, Emmanuel Todd, *Le Rendez-vous des civilizations* (Paris: Seuil, 2007), which laid out the case for demographic shifts transforming the Arab world, equated modernization with eventual democratization, and presented political ideology and culture as reflections of underlying population shifts.

11   William Sewell's early responses to Theda Skocpol remain the most interesting theoretical-cum-empirical statements of a more cultural approach to revolution. Writing in the context of conflict theory, Marxist revival, and newly institutionalist readings of Weber, Skocpol had set out the basic premises of a materialist emphasis on political-economy and state violence in Theda Skocpol, *States and Social Revolutions* (New York, NY: Cambridge University Press, 1979), modifying her position only to acknowledge ideology as an intentional manipulation of ideas in response to the religious revolution in Iran ("Rentier State and Shi'a Islam in the Iranian Revolution," *Theory and Society*, 11 [1982]: 265–303). Influenced by Geertz and the semiotic turn in French historiography, Sewell (William Sewell, "Ideologies and Social Revolutions: Reflections on the French Case," *Journal of Modern History*, 57: 1 [1985]: 57–85 and William Sewell, "Historical Events as Transformations of Structures: Inventing Revolution at the Bastille," *Theory and Society*, 25: 6 [1996]: 841–81) polemically challenged Skocpol's perspective, describing the French revolution as an "act of epoch-making cultural creativity" and "a momentous … act of signification" (Sewell, "Historical Events," 852, 861). In the decades since, with the marked diminution of academic interest in revolution, the sociological literature has been pulled between abstract theoretical affirmations of cultural causation (e.g. Jack A. Goldstone, "Ideology, Cultural Frameworks, and the Process of Revolution," *Theory and Society*, 20: 4 [1991]: 405–53; Mustafa Emirbayer and Jeff Goodwin, "Symbols, Positions, Objects: Toward a New Theory of Revolutions and Collective Action," *History and Theory*, 35: 3 [1996]: 358–74) and concrete, historical examples of cultural effects (e.g. Mansoor Moaddel, "Ideology as Episodic Discourse: The Case of the Iranian Revolution," *American Sociological Review*, 57: 3 [1992]: 353–70; Jean-Pierre Reed, "Culture in Action: Nicaragua's Revolutionary Identities Reconsidered," *New Political Science*, 24: 2 [2002]: 235–63). But see the ambitious new work of Anne Kane, *Constructing Irish Nationalist Identity: Ritual and Discourse during*

*the Irish Land War, 1879–1882* (New York, NY: Palgrave Macmillan, 2011), which renews and elaborates a cultural-sociological approach.

12  For codes and narratives as the key concepts for understanding the power of relatively autonomous culture structures; for the centrality of meaning in social explanation and causation; and for a critique of the exaggerated role that non-cultural factors such as demography play in more traditional social scientific explanations, see Jeffrey C. Alexander, *The Meanings of Social Life: A Cultural Sociology* (New York, NY: Oxford University Press, 2003) and Jeffrey C. Alexander, *The Performance of Politics: Obama's Victory and the Democratic Struggle for Power* (New York, NY: Oxford, 2010). For a recent cultural-sociological approach to social suffering and its cultural narration, see Jeffrey C. Alexander and Elizabeth Butler Breese, "Introduction: On Social Suffering," in Ron Eyerman, Jeffrey C. Alexander, and Elizabeth Butler Breese (eds), *Narrating Trauma* (Boulder, CO: Paradigm, 2011).

13  In the same month that Khaled Said was tortured and murdered – June 2010 – the anti-regime protest movement established the 'We Are All Khaled Said' (WAAKS) Facebook page to honor Said as a martyr and to inspire protests in his name. It contained two pages, one in English, and one in Arabic, both of whose administrators maintained anonymity for security reasons. In the final days of that struggle, the Arab language administrator revealed his identity. Appearing on a popular satellite television program in Cairo after being released from twelve days of captivity, Wael Ghonim acknowledged that he had initiated and led the Facebook project. In the final days of the struggle, the Egyptian became a heroic figure, not only inside the nation but outside as well. For example, *Time* magazine placed him at the head of its annual list of the hundred most important people of the year. Ghonim could perform as WAAKS (Arabic) administrator only until the day of his arrest, which was on 27 January 2011; after this date, another administrator or administrators took over, and remained anonymous. After Ghonim's release from prison, he offered posts on WAAKS (Arabic), but probably did not resume the full-time administrator role.

Both WAAKS pages played central roles in the days leading up to the revolution and throughout the eighteen days of protest that marked the event itself, from 25 January to 11 February 2011. The English and Arabic pages differed substantially from one another, not only in substance but in tone. While the two administrators carefully followed one another's language postings, they did not work together and neither claimed to know the other's identity. The Arabic language page more often adopted religious idioms and its substance was more directed to immediate events, such as timing of demonstrations, advice about protective clothing and directions about where to meet. The English page was directed less to Egypt and the Arab region and more to the putative global audience, as I will elaborate in the final section of this essay. In my quotations from these WAAKS pages, grammar, spelling, and punctuation have been left as they were written, in the heat of the moment and often amidst great commotion, stress, and upheaval. The times and dates noted in the Facebook pages are those of Egypt.

14  Slackman, "In Mideast Activism."

15  Jeffrey C. Alexander, *The Civil Sphere* (New York, NY: Oxford University Press, 2006).

16  Slackman, "In Mideast Activism."

17  Slackman, "In Mideast Activism."

18  David D. Kirkpatrick and David E. Sanger, "A Tunisian-Egyptian Link that Shook Arab History," *New York Times*, 14 February 2011, A1.

19  'We Are All Khaled Said' (WAAKS, Arabic), 27 January 2011, 3.46 p.m.:

الحرية  و الرغيف.. مطلب كل مصر شريف

20  WAAKS (English), 1 February 2011, 12.54 a.m.

21  WAAKS (English), 6 February 2011, 2.14 p.m.

22  Evan Hill, "Egypt's Rooftop Revolutionaries," Al Jazeera (English), 6 February 2011, http://english.aljazeera.net/news/middleeast/2011/02/201126194730350605.html [accessed 7 March 2011].

23  Mahmoud Hussein, "Après la Tunisie, l'Egypte Cherche sa Liberté." *Le Monde*, 27 January 2011, 18.

24  Benjamin Barthe and Cécile Hennion, "La Révolte Egyptienne; 'On s'est remis à respirer normalement, la peur a disparu'," *Le Monde*, 3 February 2011, 6.

25  Barthe and Hennion, "La Révolte Egyptienne."

26  Alaa Al Aswany, "Comment: Police Alone Can't Keep Rulers in Power. Egypt's Battle Is On," *Guardian*, 28 January 2011, 38.

27  *La Repubblica*, "Scontri e Morti in Tutto l'Egitto. Il Presidente in TV: È Complotto," *La Repubblica*, 29 January 2011, http://www.repubblica. it/esteri/2011/01/29/news/scontri_e_morti_in_tutto_l_egitto_il_ presidente_in_tv_e_complotto-11795852 [accessed 22 April 2011].

28  Anthony Shadid, "Street Battle Over the Arab Future," *New York Times*, 3 February 2011, 1.

29  Bob Prail, "In the Mideast, Days of Tumult, 'To the Editor'," *New York Times*, 29 January 2011, A22.

30  Slackman, "In Mideast Activism."

31  Kareem Fahim and Mona El-Naggar, "Violent Clashes Mark Protests Against Mubarak's Rule," *New York Times*, 26 January 2011, A1.

32  David D. Kirkpatrick, "Egyptians Defiant as Military Does Little to Quash Protests," *New York Times*, 30 January 2011, 1.

33  Liz Alderman, "Arab Executives Predict Regime Change in Egypt," *New York Times*, 29 January 2011, http://www.nytimes. com/2011/01/30/business/global/30davos.html [accessed 12 June 2011].

34  David D. Kirkpatrick, "Mubarak Orders Crackdown, With Revolt Sweeping Egypt," *New York Times*, 29 January 2011, A1.

35  Kareem Fahim, "Hopes of Egyptians, Poor and Wealthy, Converge in Fight for Cairo Bridge," *New York Times*, 29 January 2011, A12.

36  Fahim, "Hopes of Egyptians."

37  Anthony Shadid, "Seizing Control of Their Lives and Wondering What's Next," *New York Times*, 30 January 2011, A1.

38  David D. Kirkpatrick and Mona El-Naggar, "Rich, Poor and a Rift Exposed by Unrest," *New York Times*, 31 January 2011, A6.

39  David D. Kirkpatrick, "Mubarak's Grip Is Shaken as Millions Are Called to Protest," *New York Times*, 1 February 2011, A1.

40  Shadid, "Street Battle Over the Arab Future."

41  Shadid, "Street Battle Over the Arab Future."

42  Al Jazeera (English), "Egypt Protestors Clash with Police," Al Jazeera (English), 25 January 2011, http://english.aljazeera.net/news/ middleeast/2011/01/201112511362207742.html [accessed 7 March 2011].

43  Walter Ambrust, "Tahrir: Shock and Awe Mubarak Style," Al Jazeera (English), 3 February 2011, http://english.aljazeera.net/indepth/opinion/2011/02/20112310224495606.html [accessed 7 March 2011].

44  Jack Shenker, "Egypt Awaits Nationwide 'Day of Revolution'," *Guardian*, 25 January 2011, 22.

45  Ahdaf Soueif, "Fittingly, It's the Young of the Country Who Are Leading Us," *Guardian*, 28 January 2011, 1.

46  Guido Rampoldi, "La Rivolta che Cambia la Storia Araba," *La Repubblica*, 29 January 2011, http://www.repubblica.it/esteri/2011/01/29/news/la_rivolta_che_cambia_la_storia_araba-11796023 [accessed 22 April 2011].

47  WAAKS (Arabic), 27 January 2011, 9.23 p.m.:

الكنيسة المصرية تجعو المسيحيين لحضور المظاهرات السلمية مع إخوتهم المسلمين ... الحمد لله و كلنا ايد واحدة لأن كلنا عايزين حقوقنا.

48  WAAKS (Arabic), 26 January 2011.:

سنخرج بمسيرات في كل مساجد وكنائس مصر الكبرى متجهين ناحية الميادين العامة ومعتصمين حتى ننال حقوقنا المسلوبة. مصر ستخرج مسلميها ومسيحييها من أجل محاربة الفساد والبطالة والظلم وغياب الحرية. سيتم تحديد المساجد والكنائس ليلة الخميس.

49  Al Jazeera (Arabic), 25 January 2011, 7.43 a.m., http://www.aljazeera.net/NR/exeres/B0C28F6C-8BFB-4786-B183-FFFB488C956E.htm [accessed 12 June 2011].

50  Al Jazeera (Arabic) , 25 January 2011, 7.43 a.m., http://www.aljazeera.net/NR/exeres/B0C28F6C-8BFB-4786-B183-FFFB488C956E.htm [accessed 12 June 2011].

51  Soumaya Ghannoushi, "Comment: A Quagmire of Tyranny: Arabs Are Rebelling not Just against Decrepit Autocrats but the Foreign Backers Who Kept Them in Power," *Guardian*, 29 January 2011, 32.

52  Thomas Friedman, "Speakers' Corner on the Nile," *New York Times*, 8 February 2011, A27.

53  Maureen Dowd, "Stars and Sewers," *New York Times*, 20 February 2011, "Week in Review", 11.

54  At the heart of the institutions and interactions of a civil society –

even one in *status nascendi* – is a binary discourse that contrasts a sacred, purifying discourse justifying liberty with a profane, polluting discourse justifying repression. For a detailed analysis of this binary cultural structure, and its necessary if ambiguous relation to democratic aspirations, see Alexander, *The Civil Sphere*. While the specification of this cultural structure differs according to historical time and geographical place – for references to variegated historical and national studies, see Alexander, *The Civil Sphere*, 573–4 – its fundamentals are universal, insofar as they identify the kinds of motives, relations, and institutions required to sustain a self-governing democratic order. That the same discourse so clearly propelled the movement of revolutionaries in an Arab, primarily Muslim, setting provides further evidence of this universal status.

55  Michael Slackman, "Compact Between Egypt and Its Leader Erodes," *New York Times*, 29 January 2011, 11.

56  Robyn Creswell, "Egypt: The Cultural Revolution," *New York Times*, 20 February 2011, "Book Review" 27.

57  Creswell, "Egypt."

58  Slackman, "Compact Between Egypt and Its Leader Erodes."

59  The quoted phrases about the sacred and profane character of the Mubarak regime and its opponents are drawn from the regime's official press releases, from its speeches, and from anonymous, off-the-record statements to journalists. For the polluting quotations, see Slackman, "In Mideast Activism;" Fahim and El-Naggar, "Violent Clashes Mark Protests Against Mubarak's Rule;" M. Ibrahim Youssef, "Quotation of the Day," *New York Times*, 27 January 2011, A2; Mekhennet and Kulish, "With Muslim Brotherhood Set to Join Egypt Protests;" Kareem Fahim and Liam Stack, "Opposition in Egypt Gears Up for Major Friday Protest," *New York Times*, 28 January 2011, section A; David D. Kirkpatrick, "As Egypt Protest Swells, U.S. Sends Specifics Demands" *New York Times*, 9 February 2011, A1; Anthony Shadid and David D. Kirkpatrick, "Mubarak Won't Quit, Stoking Revolt's Fury and Resolve," *New York Times*, 11 February 2011, A1. For the quotes sacralizing the regime, see Fahim and Stack 2011; El-Naggar and Slackman, "Egypt's Leader Used Old Tricks;" David D. Kirkpatrick, "Mubarak Orders Crackdown;" Helene Cooper and Mark Mazzetti, "Prideful and Prizing Status Quo, Mubarak Resists Pressure," *New York Times*, 7 February 2011,

A10; Anthony Shadid, "In the Euphoria of the Crowd, No Party or Leader Unifies the Opposition," *New York Times*, 1 February 2011, A11. While drawn from quotations in the *New York Times*, these characterizations were widely reported in the other media as well, including Al Jazeera (Arabic), e.g. Al Jazeera (Arabic), 25 January 2011, 7.43 a.m., http://www.aljazeera.net/NR/exeres/B0C28F6C-8BFB-4786-B183-FFFB488C956E.htm [accessed 12 June 2011].

60  Simon Tisdall, "World Briefing: New Wave of Protest Takes Mubarak Out of Comfort Zone," *Guardian*, 26 January 2011, 22.

61  For these statements by the revolutionaries about themselves, see, e.g. David D. Kirkpatrick and Michael Slackman, "In New Role, Egypt Youths Drive Revolt," *New York Times*, 27 January 2011, A1; Fahim and Stack, "Opposition in Egypt;" Fahim, "Hopes of Egyptians." For their statements about the regime and Mubarak, see, e.g. Kareem Fahim and Liam Stack, "Egypt Intensifies Effort to Crush Wave of Protests, Detaining Hundreds," *New York Times*, 27 January 2011, A10; Mekhennet and Kulish, "With Muslim Brotherhood;" Fahim and Stack, "Opposition in Egypt", Mark Landler and Andrew W. Lehrer, "State's Secrets; Cables Show U.S. Tack on Egypt: Public Support, Private, Pressure," *New York Times*, 28 January 2011, A1; Kirkpatrick, "Mubarak Orders Crackdown;" Fahim, "Hopes of Egyptians;" David D. Kirkpatrick, "In Protests, a Nobelist Has an Unfamiliar Role," *New York Times*, 29 January 2011, A11; Neil MacFarqhar, "Egypt's Respected Military Is Seen as Pivotal in What Happens Next," *New York Times*, 29 January 2011, A13. Again, while these translated quotations are drawn from the *New York Times*, the same characterizations are widely reported, not only in American and European media but in Al Jazeera (Arabic) as well, e.g. Al Jazeera (Arabic) , 25 January 2011, 7.43 a.m., http://www.aljazeera.net/NR/exeres/B0C28F6C-8BFB-4786-B183-FFFB488C956E.htm [accessed 12 June 2011].

62  The intertwining of disillusionment with the post-colonial project and support for renewing civil society was represented in fictional form in the early 1980s by the great Egyptian novelist Naguib Mahfouz in his moral allegory: Naguib Mahfouz, *Before the Throne: Dialogs with Egypt's Great from Menes to Anwar Sadat* (Cairo: The American University in Cairo Press, 2009 [1983]). In the mythical Hall of Justice, Osiris, god of the afterlife, holds court in a trial of Egyptian rulers to determine who deserves to take a seat among the Immortals in the Hall of Sacred Justice or, instead, be consigned to

hell or purgatory. When Abdel Nasser appears before the tribunal,
he is confronted by one of his famous predecessors, Saad Zaghloul.
Nasser came to power in a 1952 military coup and championed
state socialism, pan-Arabism, anti-Zionism, and radical post-colonial
ideology. Zaghloul, Egypt's most revered revolutionary leader from
the early twentieth century, was founder of the politically and
economically liberal Wafd party. Warning that "leadership is a divine
gift," Zaghloul admonishes Nasser that "it was in your power to build
... an enlightened, democratic form of government." Nasser replies,
"true democracy to me ... meant the liberation of the Egyptians
from colonialism, exploitation, and poverty." To this, Zaghloul's
successor as Wafd leader, Mustafa al-Nahhas, angrily replies: "You
were heedless of liberty and human rights [and] while I don't deny
that you kept faith with the poor, you were a curse upon political
writers and intellectuals ... You cracked down on them with arrest
and imprisonment, with hanging and killing" (Mahfouz, *Before the
Throne*, 135–6).

63  Reuel Marc Gerecht, "How Democracy Became Halal," *New York
Times*, 7 February 2011, A23.

64  It is not an exaggeration to say that Western intellectual history
has betrayed a deep skepticism about the very possibility of Arab
democracy, from Greek tropes about Persian barbarism to Marx's
Asiatic mode of production, Weber's sultanism and warrior religion,
and the civilizational claims of such contemporary conservatives as
Samuel Huntington. Over the last three decades, this "Orientalism"
has been called out, not only by Edward Said's sweeping Foucaultian
critique (Edward Said, *Orientalism* [New York, NY: Vintage,
1979]) but by painstaking works of historical-cum-philosophical
scholarship, such as Patricia Springborg, "Politics, Primordialism,
and Orientalism: Marx, Aristotle, and the Myth of the Gemenschaft,"
*American Political Science Review*, 80: 1 [1986]: 185–211) and
Patricia Springborg, *Western Republicanism and the Oriental Prince*
[London: Polity, 1992]). It was during this same period that important
currents in Arab intellectual life initiated a far-reaching break with
"Occidentalism," the defensive mirror image of Orientalism that,
especially with the rise of the anti-colonial movement, denigrates
various elements of Western modernity, especially those having to
do with civil society and democracy. As state communism crumbled
abroad and Pan-Arab socialism foundered at home, Islamicism

certainly continued to provide for some in North Africa and the Middle East an Occidentalist alternative. There also emerged, however, a new openness, a new grappling with Western intellectual traditions and, most remarkably, with the idea of civil society. Almost two decades ago, al-Azmeh (A. al-Azmeh, *Democracy without Democrats: The Renewal of Politics in the Arab World* [London: I.B. Tauris, 1994]) already observed "the ubiquity of Arab discourse on democracy in recent years," how "together with ... the notion of civil society [it] is addressed in the Arab world in a myriad of political, academic, journalist and other writings," and how it "is the subject of inveterate commentary in casual conversation." Two years after that, in Michelle L. Browers, *Democracy and Civil Society in Arab Political Thought: Transcultural Possibilities* (Syracuse, NY: Syracuse University Press, 2006), Browers documented that among Arabic intellectuals "in the latter part of the 1980s, a literally new term entered on the scene – civil society (*al-mujtama' al-madani*)," and along with it "a constellation of concepts that radically altered the available tools of political discourse, opening up unforeseen possibilities for political thought and action." Browers demonstrated that what civil society means is highly contested among Arab intellectuals, yet, as she also pointed out, the term has been highly contested from the very beginnings of Western intellectual life as well (cf., Alexander, *The Civil Sphere*). In the Arab world, for example, more communal Islamic approaches have been contrasted, favorably and unfavorably, with definitions that emphasize more individualistic and pluralistic understandings of civil society, whether liberal or socialist. Browers concludes, nonetheless, that "the polarization between advocates of secularism and advocates of Islamicization belies an underlying consensus about at least some of the ideational constellations that construct a liberal public sphere (democracy, civil society, citizenship)" and that "despite the variation among particular conceptions of civil society there is broad agreement that enlarging a democratically engaged public sphere must be a priority for the development of the Arab region" (Browers, *Democracy and Civil Society*, 209). In the most recently published book-length examination of contemporary Egypt, *Egypt on the Brink*, Tarek Osman finds such intellectual developments paralleled by trends in the nation's popular culture: "Formulating their own definition of Egyptianism" and "depressed by the devastating decline of Egyptian culture, values, attitudes and behavior," young Egyptians "leapt over the past fifty years (seeing only troubles and failures), and embraced Egypt's liberal experiment of the 1920s, 1930s and 1940s" (Tarek Osman, *Egypt on the Brink: From Nasser to Mubarak* [New Haven, CT: Yale University Press, 2010, 210). Osman reports that "the 2000s saw a plethora of films, TV series and novels glorifying and extolling the liberal experiment, especially its tolerant values, and its relaxed modus vivendi," and he notes also the "rise of private universities, businessmen associations, chambers of commerce, consumer protection groups and the multitude of independent press and [satellite] TV channels" (Osman, *Egypt on the Brink*, 220).

It represented a remarkable lapse in the mass media reporting on the Arab Spring in general, and on the Egyptian Revolution in particular, that scarcely any mention was made of the Arab intellectual revolution of the preceding decades. This neglect reflects the broader failures of Western commentary to highlight the cultural nature of the Egyptian revolution and of Western social scientists to put meaning at the center of their analysis of revolutions. For singular academic efforts demonstrating the decisive role shifting intellectual traditions play in revolutions, see Bernard Bailyn, *The Ideological Origins of the American Revolution* (Cambridge, MA: Harvard University Press, 1967) and Keith Michael Baker, *Inventing the French Revolution: Essays in French Political Culture in the 18th Century* (Cambridge, UK: Cambridge University Press, 1990).

65  *USA Today*, "Anti-Mubarak Protest Brings Moment of Truth for US," *USA Today*, 31 January 2011, 8A.

66  Rampoldi, "La Rivolta che Cambia la Storia Araba."

67  Rampoldi, "La Rivolta che Cambia la Storia Araba."

68  Rampoldi, "La Rivolta che Cambia la Storia Araba."

69  Essam El-Errian, "What the Muslim Brothers Want," *New York Times*, 10 February 2011, A25. El-Errian is identified by the *New York Times* as a member of the Muslim Brotherhood's "guidance council" in Egypt.

70  Al Jazeera (Arabic), 25 January 2011, 7.43 a.m., http://www.aljazeera. net/NR/exeres/B0C28F6C-8BFB-4786-B183-FFFB488C956E.htm [accessed 12 June 2011].

71  Owen Dorell and Alice Fordham, "Fury Grows in Egypt," *USA Today*,

11 February 2011, 1A.

72  Thomas L. Friedman, "Up with Egypt," *New York Times*, 9 February 2011, A27.

73  Kirkpatrick and Slackman, "In New Role."

74  Kareem Fahim, "Hopes of Egyptians."

75  El-Naggar and Slackman, "Egypt's Leader Used Old Tricks."

76  Shadid, "Seizing Control of Their Lives."

77  Al-Bushra, "Egyptian Revolution."

78  Friedman, "Speakers' Corner."

79  Hamza Hendawi, "Egyptian Protesters Denounce Mubarak; Clash with Riot Police," Associated Press, 25 January 2011, http://www.aolnews.com/2011/01/25/egyptians-denouncemubarak-clash-with-riot-police [accessed 7 March 2011].

80  Mohamed ElBaradei, "The Next Step for Egypt's Opposition," *New York Times*, 11 February 2011, A27.

81  El-Naggar and Slackman, "Egypt's Leader Used Old Tricks."

82  Shadid, "Seizing Control of Their Lives."

83  Jack Shenker, "Mubarak Regime in Crisis as Biggest Anti-government Demonstrations in a Generation Sweep across Egypt," *Guardian*, 26 January 2011.

84  WAAKS (Arabic), 27 January 2011, 12.42 a.m.:

لن ترهبنا عصيانكم ولا رصاصاتكم المطاطية ولا رصاصكم الحى.. كلنا سنموت لتحيا مصر

85  Al Jazeera (Arabic), 5 February 2011, http://www.youtube.com/watch?v=wkvzYY_Kp7c&feature=relmfu&safety_mode=true&persist_safety_mode=1.

86  Michael Slackman, "A Brittle Leader, Appearing Strong," *New York Times*, 12 February 2011, A1.

87  Mekhennet and Kulish, "With Muslim Brotherhood Set to Join Egypt Protests."

88  David D. Kirkpatrick, "Egypt Protests Continue as Government Resigns," *New York Times*, 29 January 2011, http://warsclerotic.wordpress.com/2011/01/29/egypt-protests-continue-as-government-resigns-nytimes-com [accessed 20 June 2011].

89  Slackman, "In Mideast Activism."

90  Kirkpatrick and Slackman, "In New Role."

91  Thomas L. Friedman, "Pharaoh Without a Mummy," *New York Times*, 16 February 2011, A25.

92  Slackman, "In Mideast Activism."

93  Saad Eddin Ibrahim, "Mubarak's Interests Are Not America's; The Dictator Can't be Trusted," *Wall Street Journal* (online), 8 February 2011, http://online.wsj.com/article/SB1000142405274870485840457612845051161197O.html [accessed 20 June 2011].

94  Marc Champion, "In a Flash, Alexandria Erupts in Mass Jubilee," *Wall Street Journal* (online), 11 February 2011, http://online.wsj.com/article/SB10001424052748704329104576138353660891850.html [accessed 20 June 2011].

95  Bernardo Valli, "Egitto, Nella Piazza che Grida 'Da qui non ce ne andiamo'," *La Repubblica*, 5 February 2011, http://www.repubblica.it/esteri/2011/02/05/news/egitto_nella_piazza_che_grida_da_qui_non_ce_ne_andiamo-12081033 [accessed 22 April 2011].

96  Bernardo Valli, "La Beffa Finale del Faraone di Plastica," *La Repubblica*, 11 February 2011, http://www.repubblica.it/esteri/2011/02/11/news/beffa_faraone-12321773 [accessed 22 April 2011].

97  Al Jazeera (Arabic), 25 January 2011, 7.43 a.m., http://www.aljazeera.net/NR/exeres/B0C28F6C-8BFB-4786-B183-FFFB488C956E.htm [accessed 12 June 2011].

98  Peter Beaumont and Jack Shenker, "A Day of Fury: Cairo in Flames as Cities Become Battlegrounds," *Guardian*, 29 January 2011, 2.

99  Fahim and El-Naggar, "Violent Clashes Mark Protests Against Mubarak's Rule."

100  Cécile Hennion, "Egypte: Moubarak Sous Oression," *Le Monde*, 29 January 2011, 1.

101  Fabio Scuto, "El Baradei, l'Uomo del Destino 'Oggi Nasce un Paese Nuovo'," *La Repubblica*, 1 February 2011, http://www.repubblica.it/esteri/2011/02/01/news/baradei_uomo_destino-11904735 [accessed 15 April 2011].

102  This distinction can be made only if the civil sphere and the nation-state are made analytically distinct. A common error of "nationalism studies" is to explain cultural identities entirely in terms of varieties of nationalism. But the civil sphere is a relatively independent world of culture and social organization, which has its own discourse

and modes of incorporation, even as enforcement is related to state functions. To suggest that Egyptians were embracing civic as compared to primordial nationalism points to their aspiration to construct a civil sphere that was relatively independent, not only from state coercion but from religious qualifications, ethnicity, regional, and economic statuses as well.

103  Here and in later sections, the extracts that have quotation marks are statements by participants; the remainder are quotations from media observations.

104  Shadid, "Seizing Control of Their Lives."

105  David D. Kirkpatrick and David E. Sanger, "Egypt Officials Seek to Nudge Mubarak Out," *New York Times*, 5 February 2011, A1.

106  Kareem Fahim, "Birthplace of Uprising Welcomes Its Success," *New York Times*, 12 February 2011, A9.

107  Barthe and Hennion, "La Révolte Egyptienne."

108  Al Jazeera (English), "Fresh Anti-government Protests in Egypt," Al Jazeera (English), 26 January 2011, http://english.aljazeera.net/news/middleeast/2011/01/201112663450547321.html [accessed 7 March 2011].

109  Zeinab Mohamed, Victoria Hazou, David Degner, Firas al-Atraqchi and Joseph Mayton, "The Word on the Street: The Protests This Week in Egypt Against the Mubarak Regime Have Gripped the Country," *Guardian*, 28 January 2011, "G2" 6.

110  Ahdaf Soueif, "Protesters Reclaim the Spirit of Egypt," BBC News, 13 February 2011, http://www.bbc.co.uk/news/world-middle-east-12393795 [accessed 22 April 2011].

111  Kareem Fahim and Mona El-Naggar, "Emotions of a Reluctant Hero Inject New Life Into the Protest Movement," *New York Times*, 9 February 2011, A14.

112  Behind these near-term collective representations, the political culture of the movement's secular and religious leaders – in Gramsci's terms, the movement's "organic" and "high" intellectuals – remains to be further be explored. If one looked more deeply into shifting Islamic themes about freedom, justice, and community, one would undoubtedly find hyphenations between the religious and secular, recalling the kinds of amalgamations that were made, centuries ago, between Christianity and secular political ideologies

during the English and American revolutions. For the American case, see Ruth Bloch, *Visionary Republic: Millennial Themes in American Thought, 1756–1800* (New York, NY: Cambridge University Press, 1985) and Nathan C. Hatch, *The Sacred Cause of Liberty* (New Haven, CT: Yale University Press, 1977); for the British, see Michael Walzer, *The Revolution of the Saints* (Cambridge, MA: Harvard University Press, 1965).

113  See Ron Eyerman and Andrew Jameson, *Social Movements: A Cognitive Approach* (London: Polity, 1991) and Ron Eyerman, "Performing Opposition or, How Social Movements Move," in Jeffrey C. Alexander, Bernhard Giesen and Jason Mast (eds), *Social Performance: Symbolic Action, Cultural Pragmatics, and Ritual* (New York, NY: Cambridge University Press, 2006), 193–216.

114  David D. Kirkpatrick, "Protest's Old Guard Falls in Behind the Young," *New York Times*, 31 January 2011, A1.

115  Kirkpatrick, "Protest's Old Guard".

116  Ian Black, "Middle East: Protest Plans: Leaflets Being Circulated in Cairo Give Blueprint for Mass Action," *Guardian*, 28 January 2011, 26.

117  Kareem Fahim, "Hopes of Egyptians."

118  David D. Kirkpatrick, "Wired, Educated and Shrewd, Young Egyptians Guide Revolt," *New York Times*, 10 February 2011, 1.

119  For the long political-cum-conceptual history of new class ideas, see Lawrence Peter King and Iván Szelenyi, *Theories of the New Class: Intellectuals and Power* (Minneapolis, MN: University of Minnesota Press, 2004).

120  For the idea that a "culture of critical discourse" is specific to the new class, see Alvin W. Gouldner, *The Future of Intellectuals and the Rise of the New Class* (New York, NY: Seabury, 1979).

121  In analyses of the Arab Spring as it was unfolding, Farhad Khosrokhavar tellingly employed the new class trope in a less economistic manner (see Farhad Khosrokhavar, "Fin des Dictatures au Proche et Moyen-Orient? *Le Monde* (online), 17 January 2011, http://www.lemonde.fr/idees/article/2011/01/17/fin-des-dictatures-au-proche-et-moyen-orient_1466683_3232.html [accessed 12 June 2011]; Farhad Khosrokhavar, "Les Neuf Piliers de la Révolution Arabe, *Le Nouvel Observateur*, 10–16 February 2011, 94–5). Writing of "the emergence of the new middle classes" as providing "political

and moral direction," his usage is close to the concept of carrier group deployed here. Understanding revolutionary leadership as a carrier group, rather than as a representative of a class, clarifies that the leadership represents not only its own interest, or even interests per se, but broader cultural and political aspirations that are not only specific to a particular time and place but extend to groups other than their own. For an enduring study of the relation between Puritan clergy and English gentry, which together constituted the carrier group for the English Revolution, see Walzer, *The Revolution of the Saints*.

122   David D. Kirkpatrick and David E. Sanger, "A Tunisian-Egyptian Link."

123   While speaking of the organizers as a group, one should not reify the network that linked people who comprised the revolutionary leadership. At various times from 2005 onward, there were a number of associations with overlapping memberships, and shifting coalitions emerged even during the eighteen days of the revolution itself. In his field notes, for example, Atef Said notes that on "the 30th of January or so, one of the main coalitions was formed" and that "this include[d] many youth organizations who called for the protests on January 25th." It was the Coalition for the Youth of the Revolution, and included "justice and freedom (leftist), the 6th of April (liberally oriented), el Baradie supporters (liberally oriented), Muslim Brotherhood (moderate political Islamist), the youth of the Democratic Front Party (liberally oriented) ... The Coalition had a Facebook page and its press releases were circulated widely" (Atef Said, "On the Communication During the Internet Blackout in Egypt and Generally During the 18 Days of the Egyptian Revolution," Ethnographic Field Notes, unpublished manuscript, 22 April 2011). See also Maryam Ishani, "The Hopeful Network," in Marc Lynch, Susan B. Glasser, and Blake Hounshell (eds), *Revolution in the Arab World* (Washington DC: Foreign Policy, 2011). Yet, if the carrier group was more network than central committee, in the days after the Jasmine revolution in Tunisia a fairly well-organized directing group did form in Egypt, providing the strategic and tactical organization for the 25 January Revolution. In the years to come, debates will undoubtedly flourish about the history and sociology of the groups and interests constituting this revolutionary leadership and their ideologies. Hossam El-Hamalawy ("Egypt's Revolution Has Been Ten Years in the Making," *Guardian*, 2 March 2011, http://www.

guardian.co.uk/commentisfree/2011/mar/02/egypt-revolution-mubarak-wall-of-fear [accessed 10 June 2011]) and Atef Said (Atef Said, "Uprising in Egypt: America in the Egyptian Revolution," The Immanent Frame [blog], 4 April 2011, http://blogs.ssrc.org/tif/2011/04/11/america-in-the-egyptian-revolution [accessed 15 June 2011]) for example, emphasize antecedent political events going back to 2000, and claim that labor activism and "anti-imperialist" (anti-Israeli occupation, anti-American) ideology played significant, even foundational roles. In the present essay, I place more weight on developments that were discontinuous with earlier forms of Egyptian and Middle-Eastern protest: the broadly cross-class, civil-society character of the 25 January movement; the transforming effects of the intellectual revolution in Arab society; the incorporation of non-violence as a tactic; and, more broadly, the emergent properties of civil solidarity as a performative accomplishment.

124  For the relation between young Egyptian organizers and the non-violent movement in Serbia that Otpor initiated, and an analysis of the international outreach of CANVAS, the Center for Applied Non-Violent Action and Strategy, that Otpor's founders created in 2003 in Belgrade, see Tina Rosenberg, "Revolution U," in Lynch *et al.*, *Revolution in the Arab World.*

125  Ron Nixon, "U.S. Groups Helped Nurture Arab Opposition," *New York Times*, 15 April 2011, A1.

126  Words with meanings are merely locutionary, in John L. Austin's terms (John L. Austin, *How to Do Things with Words* [Cambridge, MA: Harvard University Press, 2nd edition, 1962]), but actually doing things with words indicates that speech acts go "beyond" meaning to having illocutionary or even perlocutionary effect. Illocutionary suggests the audience takes on a deep understanding of the implications of the speech, perlocutionary that the hearer takes action in response to this understanding. There are, of course, gradients. In China today, free speech is relatively protected inside of private spheres and certain institutional spaces, such as elite universities, but it is increasingly restricted in public spaces. The effect is to allow locutionary but not illocutionary or perlocutionary action – in my terms, to allow scripts to be written but to prevent them from being performed.

127  Austin, *How to Do Things with Words*.

128  Douglas B. Holt, *How Brands Become Icons: The Principles of Cultural Branding* (Boston, MA: Harvard Business School, 2004).

129  Kirkpatrick and Sanger, "A Tunisian-Egyptian Link."

130  Valentin Rauer, "Symbols in Action: Willy Brandt's Kneefall at the Warsaw Memorial," in Alexander *et al.*, *Social Performance*, 257–82.

131  Kirkpatrick, "Wired, Educated and Shrewd."

132  Kirkpatrick and Sanger, "A Tunisian-Egyptian Link."

133  Kareem Fahim and Mona El-Naggar, "Across Egypt, Protests Direct Fury at Leader," *New York Times*, 26 January 2011, A1.

134  Soueif, "Fittingly, It's the Young of the Country."

135  Slackman, "In Mideast Activism."

136  Robert D. Kaplan, "One Small Revolution," *New York Times*, 23 January 2011, "Week in Review" 11. Kaplan made his name as a neo-conservative political intellectual; he was an enthusiastic supporter of the Bush administration's invasion and occupation of Iraq.

137  Fahim and El-Naggar, "Across Egypt."

138  Jack Shenker, "Revolt Spreads to Egypt, Violent Clashes on Streets of Cairo," *Guardian*, 26 January 2011, 1.

139  Slackman, "Compact Between Egypt and Its Leader Erodes."

140  Anthony Shadid and David D. Kirkpatrick, "In Egypt, Opposition Unifies Around Government Critic," *New York Times*, 31 January 2011, 1.

141  Mohamed *et al.*, "The Word on the Street."

142  Shadid, "In the Euphoria of the Crowd."

143  Jim Michaels, "Tech-savvy Youths Led the Way in Egypt Protests; And They Want Seat at the Table in Negotiations," *USA Today*, 7 February 2011, 2A.

144  Fahim and El-Naggar, "Across Egypt."

145  Mekhennet and Kulish, "With Muslim Brotherhood."

146  Robert F. Worth, "On Al Jazeera, a Revolution Televised Despite Hurdles," *New York Times*, 29 January 2011, A11.

147  Shenker, "Revolt Spreads to Egypt."

148  *La Repubblica*, "'Mubarak Vattene. Basta Dittatura,' La Protesta degli

Egiziani a Roma," *La Repubblica*, 31 January 2011, http://roma. repubblica.it/cronaca/2011/01/31/news/mubarak_vattene_basta_ dittatura_la_protesta_degli_egiziani_a_roma-11893136 [accessed 15 April 2011]. This message was written on the signs of Egyptian protestors in Rome.

149  *Guardian*, "Front: Egypt: How the Events Unfolded," *Guardian*, 29 January 2011, 2.

150  Peter Beaumont and Jack Shenker, "Front: Egypt: A Day of Fury: Cairo in Flames as Cities Become Battlegrounds," *Guardian*, 29 January 2011, 2.

151  Harriet A. Sherwood, Angelique Chrisafis, Martin Chulov and Hazem Balousha, "Fall of Mubarak: Hope and Fear, How the Arab World Reacted," *Guardian*, 12 February 2011, 4; Gerald Seib, "Now Dawning: The Next Era of Middle East History," *Wall Street Journal* (online), 31 January 2011, http://online.wsj.com/article/SB1000142 405274870425430457611611011059 6324.html [accessed 20 June 2011]; John Bussey, "How to Handle Employee Activism: Google Tiptoes Around Cairo's Hero," *Wall Street Journal* (online), 10 February 2011, http://online.wsj.com/article/SB10001424052748704 13220457613632307358 9858.html [accessed 20 June 2011].

152  Dorell and Fordham, "Fury Grows in Egypt."

153  Shadid, "Seizing Control of Their Lives."

154  Levinson and Dagher, "Rallies Fan Out;" cf., *Guardian*, "Front: Egypt."

155  Robert Tait, "Front: Egypt: 28 Hours in the Dark Heart of Egypt's Torture Machine," *Guardian*, 10 February 2011, 4.

156  Fouad Ajami, "Egypt's 'Heroes With No Names'; We Must Remember that Mohamed Atta and Ayman Zawahiri Were Bred in the Tyranny of Hosni Mubarak," *Wall Street Journal* (online), 12 February 2011, http://online.wsj.com/article/SB100014240527487041322045761 36442019920256.html [accessed 20 June 2011].

157  *New York Times*, 4 February 2011, A12.

158  Kirkpatrick, "Egyptians Defiant."

159  Mohamed *et al.*, "The Word on the Street."

160  Fahim and El-Naggar, "Across Egypt."

161  El-Naggar and Slackman, "Egypt's Leader Used Old Tricks."

162  Marc Landler, "Obama Cautions Embattled Egyptian Ally Against Violent Repression," *New York Times*, 29 January 2011, A1.

163  Neil MacFarquhar, "Egypt's Respected Military Is Seen as Pivotal in What Happens Next," *New York Times*, 29 January 2011, A13.

164  Nicholas Kulish and Souad Mekhennet, "In Alexandria, Protesters Win After a Day of Fierce Fighting with Riot Police," *New York Times*, 29 January 2011, A12.

165  Rampoldi, "La Rivolta che Cambia la Storia Araba."

166  Michael Slackman, "Omar Suleiman: A Choice Likely to Please the Military, not the Crowds," *New York Times*, 30 January 2011, A10. The quotation is from Mahmoud Shokry, former ambassador to Syria and personal friend of Omar Suleiman, on Mr. Suleiman's appointment as vice-president.

167  Shadid, "Seizing Control of Their Lives."

168  Shadid, "Seizing Control of Their Lives."

169  Ahdaf Soueif, "Egypt: 'For Everyone Here, There's No Turning Back'," *Guardian*, 2 February 2011, 1.

170  Joshua Yaffa, "Downloading the Uprising; Can Technology's Tools Liberate Those Living Under Political Repression?" *Wall Street Journal* (online), 4 February 2011, http://online.wsj.com/article/SB10001424052748704150104576122751785029870.html [accessed 20 June 2011].

171  Anthony Shadid, "Discontented Within Egypt Face Power of Old Elites," *New York Times*, 5 February 2011, A7.

172  Owen Dorell, "Protests Have Economic Ripple Effects; Movement Gets Mixed Reviews from Those Who Aren't Taking Part as Tourism has Disappeared," *USA Today*, 7 February 2011, 4A.

173  Ian Black, "Egypt: Analysis. Constitution at the Heart of Change in Egypt," *Guardian*, 8 February 2011, 22.

174  Anthony Shadid, "Egypt's Leaders Seek to Project Air of Normalcy," *New York Times*, 8 February 2011, A1.

175  Matt Bradley, Christopher Rhoads and Shereen El Gazzar, "Cairo Demonstrators Dig In," *Wall Street Journal* (online), 8 February 2011, http://online.wsj.com/article/SB10001424052748704364004576131560748488384.html [accessed 20 June 2011].

176  *New York Times*, "Mr. Suleiman's Empty Promises," *New York Times*, 9 February 2011, A26.

177  Jack Shenker, "Teargas and Baton Charges Sweep Protesters Off Cairo's Streets," *Guardian*, 26 January 2011, 22.

178  Kirkpatrick, "Mubarak's Grip Is Shaken."

179  *New York Times*, "Beyond Mubarak," *New York Times*, 2 February 2011, A22.

180  Jack Shenker, Peter Beaumont, Ian Black, and Chris McGreal, "Egypt: Power to the People: Mubarak Finally Bows to the Inevitable," *Guardian*, 2 February 2011, 1.

181  Kareem Fahim and Mona El-Naggar, "Some Fear a Street Movement's Leaderless Status May Become a Liability," *New York Times*, 4 February 2011, A7.

182  *Le Monde*, "Le Régime Moubarak Contre-attaque," *Le Monde*, 4 February 2011, 1.

183  Valli, "Egitto, Nella Piazza che Grida."

184  Alessandra Stanley, "As Crisis Plays Out Live on TV, Commentators Hurl Brickbats at One Another," *New York Times*, 5 February 2011, A7.

185  *La Repubblica*, "Manifestanti Ancora in Piazza al Cairo Usa Premono per Cambiamento," *La Repubblica*, 5 February 2011, http://www.repubblica.it/esteri/2011/02/05/news/sostituiti_vertici_partito_mubarak_lascia-12100571 [accessed 22 April 2011].

186  David Sanger, "As Mubarak Digs In, Complications for U.S. Policy," *New York Times*, 6 February 2011, A12.

187  Shadid, "Egypt's Leaders."

188  Kirkpatrick, "As Egypt Protest Swells."

189  Valli, "La Beffa Finale."

190  Mona El-Naggar, "The Legacy of 18 Days in Tahrir Square," *New York Times*, 20 February 2011, "Week in Review" 4.

191  Al Jazeera (English), "Egypt Protesters Clash with Police," Al Jazeera (English), 25 January 2011, http://english.aljazeera.net/news/middleeast/2011/01/201112511362207742.html [accessed 7 March 2011].

192  Friedman, "Speakers' Corner."

193  Anthony Shadid, "Yearning for Respect, Arabs Find a Voice," *New York Times*, 30 January 2011, A10.

194  Niccolo Machiavelli, *The Discourses*, in *The Essential Writings of Niccolo Machiavelli*, translated and edited by Peter Constantine (New York, NY: Modern Library, 2007 [1531]), Bk I: 25.

195  Anthony Shadid, "Egypt Officials Widen Crackdown; US in Talks for Mubarak to Quit," New York Times, 4 February 2011, A1.

196  Shadid and Kirkpatrick, "In Egypt."

197  Shadid and Kirkpatrick, "In Egypt."

198  Dorell, "Protests Have Economic Ripple Effects."

199  Benjamin Barthe, "A Zamalek, la Bourgeoisie du Caire Défend ses Biens et Prend ses Distance avec le Régime," Le Monde, 1 February 2011, 6.

200  Shadid and Kirkpatrick, "In Egypt."

201  Shadid and Kirkpatrick, "In Egypt."

202  Dorell, "Protests Have Economic Ripple Effects."

203  Shadid and Kirkpatrick, "In Egypt."

204  Shadid and Kirkpatrick, "In Egypt."

205  Shadid and Kirkpatrick, "In Egypt." The director's first name is misspelled in the New York Times article. It should be Selma al-Tarzi, not Salma.

206  Thomas Hobbes, Leviathan, or The Matter, Forme, & Power of a Common-wealth Ecclesiasticall and Civill, edited by Richard Tuck (2nd edition, Cambridge, UK: Cambridge University Press, 1996[1651]), 84.

207  La Repubblica, "Scontri e Morti."

208  Al Jazeera (English), "Timeline: Egypt's Revolution," Al Jazeera (English), 14 February 2011, http://english.aljazeera.net/news/middleeast/2011/01/201112515334871490.html [accessed 12 June 2011).

209  Kirkpatrick, "Mubarak Orders Crackdown."

210  Kirkpatrick, "Egyptians Defiant."

211  Kirkpatrick, "Mubarak Orders Crackdown."

212  Victor Turner, The Ritual Process (Chicago, IL: Aldine, 1969). Jill Dolan connects Turner's ideas to contemporary performance theory and to the radical political imagination in her book, Jill Dolan, Utopia in Performance: Finding Hope at the Theater (Ann Arbor, MI: University of Michigan Press, 2005).

213  Mohamed ElBaradei, "Quotation of the Day," New York Times, 31 January 2011, A2.

214  Barthe and Hennion, "La Révolte Egyptienne."

215  Barthe and Hennion, "La Révolte Egyptienne."

216  Mohamed *et al.*, "The Word on the Street."

217  Beaumont and Shenker, "Front: Egypt."

218  Rampoldi, "La Rivolta che Cambia la Storia Araba."

219  Shadid, "Seizing Control of Their Lives."

220  Shadid, "Seizing Control of Their Lives."

221  Shadid, "Yearning for Respect."

222  *USA Today*, "Anti-Mubarak Protest."

223  *Guardian*, "Egypt: Beyond Mubarak," *Guardian*, 2 February 2011, 32.

224  Shadid, "In the Euphoria of the Crowd."

225  *New York Times*, "From Sadat to Mubarak: A Reminiscence, and a Prayer," *New York Times*, 3 February 2011, http://www.nytimes.com/2011/02/03/opinion/lweb03cairo.html [accessed 12 June 2011].

226  Cécile Hennion, "La Révolte Egyptienne; Venus en Famille, les Manifestants ont Donné à la Place Tahrir un Air de Kermesse." *Le Monde*, 3 February 2011, 5.

227  David Feith, "Democracy's Tribune on the Arab Awakening," *Wall Street Journal* (online), 4 February 2011, http://online.wsj.com/article/SB10001424052748704150104576122882240386172.html [accessed 20 June 2011].

228  Jack Shenker and Mustafa Khalili, "Day of No Departure: Cairo's Biggest Turnout Yet, but Mubarak Clings On," *Guardian*, 5 February 2011, 1.

229  Anthony Shadid, "At Night in Tahrir Square, Cairo Protest Gives Way to Poetry and Performances," *New York Times*, 7 February 2011, A9.

230  Friedman, "Speakers' Corner."

231  Mimi Hall and Kevin Johnson, "White House Pushes for 'genuine transition'; 'Fast-changing situation' in Egypt Difficult to Track," *USA Today*, 11 February 2011, 1A.

232  *New York Times*, "Egypt's Moment," *New York Times*, 12 February 2011, A20.

233  Anthony Shadid, "After Tahrir, Uncharted Ground," *New York Times*, 12 February 2011, A1.

234  Nicholas D. Kristoff, "Exhilarated by the Hope in Cairo," *New York Times*, 1 February 2011, A27.

235  Shadid, "At Night in Tahrir Square."

236  Barthe and Hennion, "La Révolte Egyptienne."

237  Shadid, "At Night in Tahrir Square."

238  Matt Bradley, "Rioters Jolt Egyptian Regime," *Wall Street Journal* (online), 25 January 2011, http://online.wsj.com/article/SB1000142 4052748704698004576104112320465414.html [accessed 20 June 2011].

239  Soueif, "Fittingly, It's the Young of the Country."

240  Shadid, "At Night in Tahrir Square."

241  Barthe and Hennion, "La Révolte Egyptienne."

242  Al Jazeera (English), "Tahrir: the Epicenter of the Revolution," Al Jazeera (English), 7 February 2011, http://www.youtube.com/ watch?v=SeTzu9aK3xs [accessed 7 March 2011].

243  Gregg Carlstrom, "Community Amid Egypt's Chaos," Al Jazeera (English), 7 February 2011, http://english.aljazeera.net/news/ middleeast/2011/02/201127162644461244.html [accessed 7 March 2011].

244  Cécile Hennion, "Sur la Place Tahrir, Epicentre de la Révolte Egyptienne," *Le Monde*, 1 February 2011, 6.

245  Shadid and Kirkpatrick, "In Egypt."

246  Shadid, "In the Euphoria of the Crowd."

247  El-Naggar, "The Legacy." El-Naggar refers here to an encounter two weeks earlier.

248  Anthony Shadid, "Mubarak Won't Run Again, But Stays; Obama urges a Faster Shift of Power," *New York Times*, 2 February 2011, A1.

249  Shadid, "Discontented Within Egypt."

250  Friedman, "Speakers' Corner."

251  The violence concentrated on 2 February but carried into the next day (Shadid, "Street Battle Over the Arab Future.")

252  C. McGreal, "Front: Egypt in Crisis: 'Mubarak is still here, but there's been a revolution in our minds'," *Guardian*, 6 February 2011, 4.

253  Theodore May, "Protesters Stand Fast in Cairo's Tahrir Square," *USA Today*, 8 February 2011, 4A.

254  Shadid, "Egypt Officials Widen Crackdown."

255  Ruba Assaf, "Thugs Confront Egyptian Protesters," Al Jazeera (Arabic)

(Read by Hatem Ghandir),4 February 2011, http://www.youtube. com/watch?v=5zX8IlGBDZ4&feature=relmfu [accessed 10 June 2011].

256  Shadid, "Egypt's Leaders."

257  Kirkpatrick, "As Egypt Protest Swells."

258  WAAKS, 8 February 2011. David D. Kirkpatrick, "Google Executive Who Was Jailed Said He Was Part of Online Campaign in Egypt," *New York Times*, 8 February 2011, A10. Translated from the Arabic by the *New York Times*.

259  Fahim and El-Naggar, "Emotions of a Reluctant Hero."

260  Kirkpatrick, "Google Executive."

261  Fahim and El-Naggar, "Emotions of a Reluctant Hero."

262  Hosni Mubarak, "I will not ... accept to hear foreign dictations," *Washington Post* (online), 10 February 2011, http://www. washingtonpost.com/wp-dyn/content/article/2011/02/10/ AR2011021005290.html [accessed 10 June 2011].

263  Shadid and Kirkpatrick, "Mubarak Won't Quit."

264  David D. Kirkpatrick, "Mubarak Out," *New York Times*, 12 February 2011, 1.

265  Ajami, "Egypt's 'Heroes With No Names'."

266  Ahdaf Soueif, "Fall of Mubarak: 'Look at the streets of Egypt ... this is what hope looks like'," *Guardian*, 12 February 2011, 2.

267  Shadid, "After Tahrir."

268  Fahim, "Birthplace of Uprising Welcomes Its Success."

269  *Wall Street Journal*, "Celebrations Follow Resignation in Egypt," *Wall Street Journal* (online), 12 February 2011, http://blogs.wsj.com/ photojournal/2011/02/11/celebrations-follow-resignation-in-egypt/ [accessed 20 June 2011].

270  Shadid, "After Tahrir."

271  Kirkpatrick and Sanger, "A Tunisian-Egyptian Link."

272  Worth, "On Al Jazeera."

273  Al-Bushra, "Egyptian Revolution."

274  Worth, "On Al Jazeera."

275  Worth, "On Al Jazeera;" Marc Lynch, "Beyond the Arab Street: Iraq and the Arab Public Sphere," *Politics and Society* 31: 1 (2003): 55–91.

Of course, mass media of communication are not the only means for dissenting discourse and drama to be displayed and distributed. Under Nazi and communist totalitarianism, underground ("*samizdat*") mimeographed and printed material circulated secretly alongside word of mouth "whispering" campaigns. In ethnographic field notes from his stay in Cairo during the latter days of the revolution, Atef Said reports that word of mouth communication was a significant response to the government's efforts at blocking digital communication: "Activists who left for their homes talked to their neighbors. Also, activists used land lines during this period, at night, to call their friends and make sure things are ok or send messages about what to do tomorrow." Said's notes also mention that, although talking to taxi drivers "is an old method," they "knew stories and they tell others stories" (Said, "On the Communication").

276   Said's field notes make clear that even when the regime's effort to blackout digital communication was its most intense level – during the two-day period 28–9 January – the attempt was never more than partially successful: "During these days both Facebook and Twitter were not working properly [but] bloggers and activists in Twitter distributed information about opening Facebook by proxy or twitter ... On 29th [January] cell-phones were back to work ... On January 30th, Google provided voice your tweet service to Egypt ... On Feb. 2nd, internet was back. During all this time, [while] al-jazeera Arabic was often subjected to disarraying [*sic*] ... Egyptians [with] a particular satellite could watch [or follow it] via the internet" (Said, "On the Communication").

277   Brian Stelter, "From Afar, News about Egypt." *New York Times*, 14 February 2011, B4.

278   Jennifer Preston, "While Facebook Plays a Star Role in the Revolts, Its Executives Stay Offstage," *New York Times*, 15 February 2011, 10.

279   Preston, "While Facebook Plays a Star Role."

280   Christine Hauser, "New Service Lets Voices from Egypt Be Heard," *New York Times*, 2 February 2011, A14.

281   Mansoura Ez-Eldin, "Date with a Revolution," *New York Times*, 31 January 2011, A19.

282   Keying on the word "Mubarak," a Stanford computer studies graduate student, Rio Akasaka, constructed a real-time "vimeo" (shared video) of worldwide social network activity from 7 to 14

February 2011. Among the 455,840 tweets whose motion he mapped, by far the highest concentration was in North America and Europe, with significant activity as well in the Middle East (see http://vimeo.com/20233225). A similar pattern of global social networking activity is revealed in Akasaka's vimeo collection of 123,000 tweets during the final minutes of Mubarak's 10 February speech, when he announced he would not resign (see http://vimeo.com/19824159). As this tweet networking map indicates, the transnational surround of Egypt's revolution very much included a regional force of more immediately contiguous countries, often referred to as the Arab public sphere (Lynch, "Beyond the Arab Street"). Culturally and politically, events in Egypt have for centuries been intertwined with such a broader Arab connection, and they are ever more closely connected in the digitalized social media world of today. The narrative of national decline and resurrection, for example, was directed as much to the restoration of Egypt's once leading place in the Arab world as it was to Egypt's place in "civilization" as such. And vice versa: Egypt's cultural and political institutions have been matters of great import to the Arab public sphere. Al Jazeera's dense and enthusiastic coverage of the Egyptian revolution was energized by these regional bonds even as it was regulated by the standards of independent journalism and global civil society.

283   The ideal of a global civil sphere captures something terribly significant about contemporary social realities, but it also fundamentally distorts them in a wish-fulfilling way (Jeffrey C. Alexander, "Globalization as Collective Representation: The New Dream of a Cosmopolitan Civil Sphere," in Ino Rossi (ed.), *Frontiers Of Globalization Research: Theoretical And Methodological Approaches* [New York, NY: Springer, 2007], 371–82). Some strands of public opinion do circulate globally, from popular and high culture to moral opinions about current events, but this collective will formation hardly possesses the wide reach of public opinion inside the civil spheres of democratic nation states. Nor can global public opinion, even in its necessarily fragmented form, be implemented by political power acting in its name. The global community has no state, no electoral process, no political party competition, and no monopoly on violence – all basic institutional prerequisites for regulating social processes on behalf of civil power.

284   Hillary Rodham Clinton, "Remarks with Spanish Foreign Minister

Trinidad Jimenez After Their Meeting," 25 January 2011, Washington, DC, http://www.state.gov/secretary/rm/2011/01/155280.htm, [accessed 10 June 2011].

285 If China's economic rise is eventually accompanied by commensurate military power – as modern Japan and Germany's postwar economic revivals were not – it may aggressively challenge Western civil definitions of "global." If China itself undergoes a democratic transition, binding its state to domestic civil power, it could have quite the opposite effect, allowing the civil definition of "global" to become more truly global in a substantive sense. This would be especially true if a new China were aligned with democracies in Japan and Korea. The glaring weakness of such realist geopolitical treatises as Paul Kennedy, *The Rise and Fall of the Great Powers* (New York, NY: Random House, 1987) or Samuel Huntington, *The Clash of Civilizations* (New York, NY: Simon & Schuster, 1996) is their failure to consider the potential affect on state interest and military power of such civil sphere binding or the lack thereof. This issue was forcefully articulated by an opinion piece in *Le Monde*: "The events in Egypt and Tunisia pose an important question to Western democracies: Should they practice public diplomacy committing themselves to 'universal' values? In sum, should they keep the flag of civil liberties and human rights in their pocket, pull it out halfway or deploy it permanently? ... The demonstrators in Cairo and Tunis send a message to the school of realist diplomacy: they must call a dictator a dictator, and loudly" (*Le Monde*, "Editorial; Il Faut Appeler un Dictateur un Dictateur," *Le Monde*, 2 February 2011, 1). While this is a forceful normative statement, however, the ideals of a global civil sphere are not universally applied and so-called realist considerations often overrule. Not every dictator is called a dictator. Neither is it the case that the internal construction of a civil society will make it behave externally in a peaceful manner. The discourse of civil society is binary and splitting, and it often sustains aggression outside the nation state even as it promotes pacific democracy at home. A post-dictatorship Egypt could be violently anti-Zionist, for example.

286 For the role of metaphor in politics, see Eric Ringmar, "The Power of Metaphor: Consent, Dissent & Revolution," in R. Mole (ed.), *Discursive Constructions of Identity in European Politics* (London: Palgrave Macmillan, 2007); for the role of performance

in the international relations between states, see Eric Ringmar, "Performing International Relations: Two East Asian Alternatives to the Westphalian Order," *International Organization* 66: 2 (2012).

287  Nicholas D. Kristoff, "Militants, Women and Tahrir Square," *New York Times*, 6 February 2011, "Week in Review" 8.

288  *New York Times*, "Beyond Mubarak."

289  Kristoff, "Militants, Women and Tahrir Square."

290  Kristoff, "Militants, Women and Tahrir Square."

291  Caroline Fourest, "Sans Détour; Le Mur du Caire Doit lomber," *Le Monde*, 5 February 2011, 20.

292  Steven Laurence Kaplan, "De 1789 à L'Intifada Egyptienne, le Pain," *Le Monde*, 8 February 2011, 19.

293  Lucio Caracciolo, "L'Occasione che Perderemo," *La Repubblica*, 31 January 2011, http://www.repubblica.it/esteri/2011/01/31/news/occasione_egitto-11862368 [accessed 22 April 2011].

294  There was variation in the speed with which media resolved the ambiguity between "1979" and "1989." In the United States, the *New York Times* moved more quickly than more conservative papers such as the *Wall Street Journal* and *USA Today*. In Europe, while the *Guardian* moved much more quickly than either *Le Monde* or *La Reppublica*, this was not because of ideological differences but because of the greater continental fear of North African instability increasing immigration. As for Al Jazeera, the news agency did not manifest ambivalence in the first place.

295  Lionel Beehner, "In Egypt, 'Islamist' Fears Overblown," *USA Today*, 1 February 2011, 7A.

296  *USA Today*, "Rumblings abroad test American ideals," *USA Today*, 27 January 2011, 8A.

297  The extraordinary consensus among these otherwise widely divergent media in their reporting of the Egyptian revolution – all of which aligned itself with the democratic aspirations of the revolutionary protagonists in Egypt – provides an operational definition of "global civil sphere." The definition of "global" is as much normative as real. At the time of this writing, the Chinese government has formally designated the Egyptian Revolution as a "sensitive subject" to which references may not be publicly made.

298  While the tone of Al Jazeera (Arabic) was often more overtly critical

than the *New York Times'*, and frequently more passionate and emotional, it contrasted less with the tone of television coverage in American and Europe. In its Arabic broadcasts, Al Jazeera also often intermingled reportage with overt "editorial" opinion, a practice more typical in European than American newspapers.

299  Al Jazeera (Arabic), 25 January 2011, 11.59 a.m., http://www.aljazeera.net/NR/exeres/35AFA009-4090-41FD-9C73-9A703FB54E12.htm [accessed 12 June 2011].

300  Al Jazeera (Arabic), 25 January 2011, 11:59 a.m., http://www.aljazeera.net/NR/exeres/35AFA009-4090-41FD-9C73-9A703FB54E12.htm [accessed 12 June 2011].

301  Jack Shenker, "Egypt: Journalist's Detention: Bloody and Bruised in the Back of a Truck, Destination Unknown." *Guardian*, 27 January 2011, 18.

302  For contemporary accounts of the Egyptian governments efforts to repress journalists during the 25 January Revolution, see Ashraf Khalil, "February 3: Sword vs. Pen", in Lynch *et al., Revolution in the Arab World*, and Hugh Miles, "The Al Jazeera Effect", in Lynch *et al., Revolution in the Arab World*.

303  Kirkpatrick, "Mubarak's Grip Is Shaken."

304  Beaumont and Shenker, "Front: Egypt."

305  *Guardian*, "Front: Egypt".

306  Beaumont and Shenker, "Front: Egypt."

307  Jack Shenker and Ian Black, "Egypt: Change is Coming, Says ElBaradei as US Calls for 'orderly transition'," *Guardian*, 31 January 2011, 1.

308  Soueif, "Egypt."

309  Julian Borger and Jack Shenker, "Egypt: Day of Rumour and Sky-high Expectations Ends in Anger and Confusion," *Guardian*, 11 February 2011, 4.

310  Dorell and Fordham, "Fury Grows in Egypt."

311  David E. Sanger, "When Armies Decide," *New York Times*, 20 February 2011, "Week in Review" 1.

312  For example: "To the Editor: While al Jazeera may have a bias toward the long-suffering downtrodden of the Arab world, its highly professional reporting is a breath of fresh air, representing journalism at its finest. It brings transparency to a part of the world that has

been burdened with far more than its share of autocratic regimes living off the backs of the poor." Tom Miller, "In the Mideast, Days of Tumult," *New York Times*, 29 January 2011, A22; "To the Editor: Why do the people of Egypt have to place themselves in danger of being shot and tear-gassed by the riot police before the United States realizes that it has a 'moral responsibility to stand with those who have the courage to oppose authoritarian rulers' (editorial, Jan. 29)? The United States government has been aware of the nature of President Hosni Mubarak's regime for decades and has sustained it through generous foreign aid, but for whose 'national security concerns'? America's or Israel's? It's time to come down off the fence and stand up for justice. What's what Americans claim they are good at, and now is the time to prove it, across the Middle East." Ibrahim Hewitt, "Sorting Out the Uprising in Egypt," *New York Times*, 1 February 2011, A26.

313  Mark Landler, "Obama Cautions Embattled Egyptian Ally."

314  Mark Landler, "Clinton Calls for 'Orderly Transition' to Greater Freedom in Egypt," *New York Times*, 31 January 2011, A6.

315  Judy Dempsey, "Key European Leaders Urge Restraint in Cairo," *New York Times*, 30 January 2011, http://www.nytimes.com/2011/01/31/world/europe/31europe.html [accessed 12 June 2011].

316  M. Landler and A. Lehren, "State's Secrets; Cables Show US Tack on Egypt: Public Support, Private Pressure," *New York Times*, 28 January 2011, A1."

317  Kirkpatrick and Sanger, "A Tunisian-Egyptian Link."

318  Kirkpatrick, "Mubarak Out."

319  Ben Zimmer, "How the War of Words Was Won." *New York Times*, 13 February 2011, "Week in Review" 4.

320  Kirkpatrick, "Egyptians Defiant."

321  Mona El-Naggar, "Egypt to End the Ubiquity of Mubarak," *New York Times*, 22 April 2011, A8.

# Bibliography

Ajami, F., "Egypt's 'Heroes With No Names'; We Must Remember that Mohamed Atta and Ayman Zawahiri Were Bred in the Tyranny of Hosni Mubarak," *Wall Street Journal* (online), 12 February 2011, http://online.wsj.com/article/SB10001424052748704132204576136442019 920256.html [accessed 20 June 2011].

Al-Azmeh, A., "Populism Contra Democracy: Recent Democratic Discourse in the Arab world," in Ghassan Salame (ed.), *Democracy without Democrats: The Renewal of Politics in the Arab World* London: I.B. Tauris, p. 112.

Al-Bushra, F., "Egyptian Revolution," Al Jazeera (Arabic), 28 January 2011, http://www.youtube.com/watch?v=JYuxjgU6yeE&feature=chan nel_video_title [accessed 10 June 2011].

Alderman, L., "Arab Executives Predict Regime Change in Egypt," *New York Times*, 29 January 2011, http://www.nytimes.com/2011/01/30/business/global/30davos.html [accessed 12 June 2011].

Alexander, J.C., *The Meanings of Social Life: A Cultural Sociology*, New York, NY: Oxford University Press, 2003.

Alexander, J.C., *The Civil Sphere*, New York, NY: Oxford University Press, 2006.

Alexander, J.C., "Globalization as Collective Representation: The New Dream of a Cosmopolitan Civil Sphere," in I. Rossi (ed.), *Frontiers Of Globalization Research: Theoretical And Methodological Approaches*, New York, NY: Springer, 2007, pp. 371–82

Alexander, J.C., *The Performance of Politics: Obama's Victory and the Democratic Struggle for Power*, New York, NY: Oxford University Press, 2010.

Alexander, J.C. and Breese, E., "Introduction: On Social Suffering," in R. Eyerman, J.C. Alexander, and E. Breese (eds), *Narrating Trauma*, Boulder, CO: Paradigm, 2011.

Al Jazeera (Arabic), 25 January 2011, 7.43 a.m., http://www.aljazeera.
net/NR/exeres/B0C28F6C-8BFB-4786-B183-FFFB488C956E.htm
[accessed 12 June 2011].

Al Jazeera (Arabic), 25 January 2011, 11.59 a.m., http://www.aljazeera.
net/NR/exeres/35AFA009-4090-41FD-9C73-9A703FB54E12.htm
[accessed 12 June 2011].

Al Jazeera (English), "Egypt Protesters Clash with Police," Al Jazeera
(English), 25 January 2011, http://english.aljazeera.net/news/
middleeast/2011/01/201112511362207742.html [accessed 7 March
2011].

Al Jazeera (English), "Fresh Anti-government Protests in Egypt," Al
Jazeera (English), 26 January 2011, http://english.aljazeera.net/news/
middleeast/2011/01/201112663450547321.html [accessed 7 March
2011].

Al Jazeera (English), "Tahrir: the Epicenter of the Revolution," Al
Jazeera (English), 7 February 2011, http://www.youtube.com/
watch?v=SeTzu9aK3xs [accessed 7 March 2011].

Al Jazeera (English), "Timeline: Egypt's Revolution," Al Jazeera
(English), 14 February 2011, http://english.aljazeera.net/news/
middleeast/2011/01/201112515334871490.html [accessed 12 June
2011).

Ambrust, W., "Tahrir: Shock and Awe Mubarak Style," Al Jazeera
(English), 3 February 2011, http://english.aljazeera.net/indepth/
opinion/2011/02/20112310224495606.html [accessed 7 March 2011].

Assaf, R., "Thugs Confront Egyptian Protesters," Al Jazeera (Arabic) (Read
by Hatem Ghandir), 4 February 2011, http://www.youtube.com/watc
h?v=5zX8IlGBDZ4&feature=relmfu [accessed 10 June 2011].

Aswany, A., "Comment: Police Alone Can't Keep Rulers in Power. Egypt's
Battle Is On," *Guardian*, 28 January 2011, p. 38.

Austin, J.L., *How To Do Things With Words*, 2nd edition, Cambridge, MA:
Harvard University Press, 1962.

Bailyn, B., *The Ideological Origins of the American Revolution*,
Cambridge, MA: Harvard University Press, 1967.

Baker, K.M., *Inventing the French Revolution: Essays in French Political
Culture in the 18th Century*, Cambridge, UK: Cambridge University
Press, 1990.

Barthe, B., "A Zamalek, la Bourgeoisie du Caire Défend ses Biens et Prend ses Distance avec le Régime," *Le Monde*, 1 February 2011, p. 6.

Barthe, B. and Hennion, C., "La Révolte Egyptienne; 'On s'est remis à respirer normalement, la peur a disparu'," *Le Monde*, 3 February 2011, p. 6.

Beaumont, P. and Shenker, J., "Front: Egypt: A Day of Fury: Cairo in Flames as Cities Become Battlegrounds," *Guardian*, 29 January 2011, p. 2.

Beehner, L., "In Egypt, 'Islamist' Fears Overblown," *USA Today*, 1 February 2011, p. 7A.

Black, I., "Middle East: Protest Plans: Leaflets Being Circulated in Cairo Give Blueprint for Mass Action," *Guardian*, 28 January 2011, p. 26.

Black, I., "Egypt: Analysis. Constitution at the Heart of Change in Egypt," *Guardian*, 8 February 2011, p. 22.

Bloch, R., *Visionary Republic: Millenial Themes in American Thought, 1756–1800*, New York, NY: Cambridge University Press, 1985.

Blow, C.M., "The Kindling of Change," *New York Times*, 5 February 2011, p. A17.

Borger, J. and Shenker, J., "Egypt: Day of Rumour and Sky-high Expectations Ends in Anger and Confusion," *Guardian*, 11 February 2011, p. 4.

Bradley, M., "Rioters Jolt Egyptian Regime," *Wall Street Journal* (online), 25 January 2011, http://online.wsj.com/article/SB1000142405274870 469800457610411232 0465414.html [accessed 20 June 2011].

Bradley, M., Rhoads, C., and El Gazzar, S., "Cairo Demonstrators Dig In," *Wall Street Journal* (online), 8 February 2011, http://online.wsj.com/ article/SB10001424052748704364004576131560748488384.html [accessed 20 June 2011].

Browers, M., *Democracy and Civil Society in Arab Political Thought: Transcultural Possibilities*, Syracuse, NY: Syracuse University Press, 2006.

Bussey, J., "How to Handle Employee Activism: Google Tiptoes Around Cairo's Hero," *Wall Street Journal* (online), 10 February 2011, http:// online.wsj.com/article/SB10001424052748704132204576136323073 589858.html [accessed 20 June 2011].

.aracciolo, L., "L'Occasione che Perderemo," *La Repubblica*, 31 January 2011, http://www.repubblica.it/esteri/2011/01/31/news/occasione_egitto-11862368 [accessed 22 April 2011].

Carlstrom, G., "Community Amid Egypt's Chaos," Al Jazeera (English), 7 February 2011, http://english.aljazeera.net/news/middleeast/2011/02/201127162644461244.html [accessed 7 March 2011].

Champion, M., "In a Flash, Alexandria Erupts in Mass Jubilee," *Wall Street Journal* (online), 11 February 2011, http://online.wsj.com/article/SB10001424052748704329104576138353660891850.html [accessed 20 June 2011].

Cooper, H. and Mazzetti, M., "Prideful and Prizing Status Quo, Mubarak Resists Pressure", *New York Times*, 7 February 2011, p. A10.

Cooper, H., Landler, M., and Mazzetti, M., "Sudden Split Recasts Foreign Policy," *New York Times*, 3 February 2011, p. A1.

Creswell, R., "Egypt: The Cultural Revolution," *New York Times*, 20 February 2011, "Book Review", p. 27.

Dempsey, J., "Key European Leaders Urge Restraint in Cairo," *New York Times*, 30 January 2011, http://www.nytimes.com/2011/01/31/world/europe/31europe.html [accessed 12 June 2011].

Dolan, J., 2005. *Utopia in Performances: Finding Hope at the Theater*, Ann Arbor, MI: University of Michigan Press.

Dorell, O., "Muslim Group Supports Protests; But Brotherhood's Rise Could Put US Interests at Risk," *USA Today*, 1 February 2011, p. 5A.

Dorell, O., "Protests Have Economic Ripple Effects; Movement Gets Mixed Reviews from Those Who Aren't Taking Part as Tourism has Disappeared," *USA Today*, 7 February 2011, p. 4A.

Dorell, O. and Fordham, A., "Fury Grows in Egypt," *USA Today*, 11 February 2011, p. 1A.

Dowd, M., "Stars and Sewers," *New York Times*, 20 February 2011, "Week in Review", p. 11.

ElBaradei, M., "Photo Caption," *New York Times*, 27 January 2011, p. A10.

ElBaradei, M., "Quotation of the Day," *New York Times*, 31 January 2011, p. A2.

ElBaradei, M., "The Next Step for Egypt's Opposition," *New York Times*, 11 February 2011, p. A27.

El-Errian, E., "What the Muslim Brothers Want," *New York Times*, 10 February 2011, p. A25.

El-Hamalawy, H., "Egypt's Revolution Has Been Ten Years in the Making," *Guardian*, 2 March 2011, http://www.guardian.co.uk/commentisfree/2011/mar/02/egypt-revolution-mubarak-wall-of-fear [accessed 10 June 2011].

El-Naggar, M., "The Legacy of 18 Days in Tahrir Square," *New York Times*, 20 February 2011, "Week in Review", p. 4.

El-Naggar, M., "Egypt to End the Ubiquity of Mubarak," *New York Times*, 22 April 2011, p. A8.

El-Naggar, M. and Slackman, M., "Egypt's Leader Used Old Tricks to Defy New Demands," *New York Times*, 28 January 2011, p. A11.

Eyerman, R., "Performing Opposition or, How Social Movements Move," in J.C. Alexander, B. Giesen and J. Mast (eds), *Social Performance: Symbolic Action, Cultural Pragmatics, and Ritual*, New York, NY: Cambridge University Press, 2006, pp. 193–216.

Eyerman, R. and Jameson, A., *Social Movements: A Cognitive Approach*, London: Polity, 1991.

Ez-Eldin, M., "Date with a Revolution," *New York Times*, 31 January 2011, p. A19.

Fahim, K., "Hopes of Egyptians, Poor and Wealthy, Converge in Fight for Cairo Bridge." *New York Times*, 29 January 2011, p. A12.

Fahim, K., "Birthplace of Uprising Welcomes Its Success," *New York Times*, 12 February 2011, p. A9

Fahim, K. and El-Naggar, M., "Across Egypt, Protests Direct Fury at Leader," *New York Times*, 26 January 2011, p. 1.

Fahim, K. and El-Naggar, M., "Violent Clashes Mark Protests Against Mubarak's Rule," *New York Times*, 26 January 2011, p. A1.

Fahim, K. and El-Naggar, M., "Some Fear a Street Movement's Leaderless Status May Become a Liability," *New York Times*, 4 February 2011, p. A7.

Fahim, K. and El-Naggar, M., "Emotions of a Reluctant Hero Inject New Life Into the Protest Movement," *New York Times*, 9 February 2011, p. A14.

Fahim, K. and Stack, L., "Egypt Intensifies Effort to Crush Wave of Protests, Detaining Hundreds," *New York Times*, 27 January 2011, p. A10.

Fahim, K. and Stack, L., "Opposition in Egypt Gears Up for Major Friday Protest," *New York Times*, 28 January 2011, section A.

Feith, D., "Democracy's Tribune on the Arab Awakening," *Wall Street Journal* (online), 4 February 2011, http://online.wsj.com/article/SB10 00142405274870415010457612288240386172.html [accessed 20 June 2011].

Fourest, C., "Sans Détour; Le Mur du Caire Doit Iomber," *Le Monde*, 5 February 2011, p. 20.

Friedman, T.L., "Speakers' Corner on the Nile," *New York Times*, 8 February 2011, p. A27.

Friedman, T.L., "Up with Egypt," *New York Times*, 9 February 2011, p. A27.

Friedman, T.L., "Pharaoh Without a Mummy," *New York Times*, 15 February 2011, p. A25.

Gerecht, R., "How Democracy Became Halal," *New York Times*, 7 February 2011, p. A23.

Gouldner, A., *The Future of Intellectuals and the Rise of the New Class*, New York, NY: Seabury, 1979.

*Guardian*, "Egypt: Rage against the Mubaraks," *Guardian*, 27 January 2011, p. 36.

*Guardian*, "Front: Egypt: How the Events Unfolded," *Guardian*, 29 January 2011, p. 2.

*Guardian*, "Egypt: Beyond Mubarak," *Guardian*, 2 February 2011, p. 32.

Ghannoushi, S., "Comment: A Quagmire of Tyranny: Arabs Are Rebelling not Just against Decrepit Autocrats but the Foreign Backers Who Kept Them in Power," *Guardian*, 29 January 2011, p. 32.

Hall, M. and Johnson, K., "White House Pushes for 'genuine transition'; 'Fast-changing situation' in Egypt Difficult to Track," *USA Today*, 11 February 2011, p. 1A.

Hauser, C. "New Service Lets Voices from Egypt Be Heard," *New York Times*, 2 February 2011, p. A14.

Hatch, N., *The Sacred Cause of Liberty*, New Haven, CT: Yale University Press, 1977.

Hendawi, H., "Egyptian Protesters Denounce Mubarak; Clash with Riot Police," Associated Press, 25 January 2011, http://www.aolnews. com/2011/01/25/egyptians-denouncemubarak-clash-with-riot-police [accessed 7 March 2011].

Hennion, C., "Un Mouvement de Contestation Gagne l'Egypte," *Le Monde*, 27 January 2011, p. 5.

Hennion, C., "Egypte: Moubarak Sous Pression," *Le Monde*, 29 January 2011, p. 1.

Hennion, C., "Sur la Place Tahrir, Epicentre de la Révolte Egyptienne," *Le Monde*, 1 February 2011, p. 6.

Hennion, C., "La Révolte Egyptienne; Venus en Famille, les Manifestants ont Donné à la Place Tahrir un Air de Kermesse." *Le Monde*, 3 February 2011, p. 5.

Hewitt, I., "Sorting Out the Uprising in Egypt. Letters," *New York Times*, 1 February 2011, p. A26.

Hill, E., "Egypt's Rooftop Revolutionaries," Al Jazeera (English), 6 February 2011, http://english.aljazeera.net/news/middleeast/2011/02/201126194730350605.html [accessed 7 March 2011].

Hobbes, T., *Leviathan, or The Matter, Forme, & Power of a Commonwealth Ecclesiasticall and Civill*, edited by Richard Tuck, 2nd edition, Cambridge, UK: Cambridge University Press, 1996 [1651].

Holt, D., *How Brands Become Icons: The Principles of Cultural Branding*, Boston, MA: Harvard Business School, 2004.

Hussein, M., "Après la Tunisie, l'Egypte Cherche sa Liberté," *Le Monde*, 27 January 2011, p. 18.

Ibrahim, S., "Mubarak's Interests Are Not America's; The Dictator Can't be Trusted," *Wall Street Journal* (online), 8 February 2011, http://online.wsj.com/article/SB10001424052748704858404576128450511611970.html [accessed 20 June 2011].

Ishani, M., "The Hopeful Network," in M. Lynch, S.B. Glasser, and B. Hounshell (eds), *Revolution in the Arab World*, Washington, DC: Foreign Policy, 2011.

Kaplan, R., "One Small Revolution," *New York Times*, 23 January 2011, "Week in Review", p. 11.

Kaplan, S., "De 1789 à L'Intifada Egyptienne, le Pain," *Le Monde*, 8 February 2011, p. 19.

Khalil, A., "February 3: Sword vs. Pen," in M. Lynch, S.B. Glasser, and B. Hounshell (eds), *Revolution in the Arab World*, Washington, DC: Foreign Policy, 2011.

Khosrokhavar, F., "Fin des Dictatures au Proche et Moyen-Orient?" *Le Monde* (online), 17 January 2011, http://www.lemonde.fr/idees/article/2011/01/17/fin-des-dictatures-au-proche-et-moyen-orient_1466683_3232.html [accessed 12 June 2011].

Khosrokhavar, F., "Les Neuf Piliers de la Révolution Arabe," *Le Nouvel Observateur*, 10–16 February 2011, pp. 94-95.

King, L.P. and Szelenyi, I., *Theories of the New Class: Intellectuals and Power*, Minneapolis, MN: University of Minnesota Press, 2004.

Kirkpatrick, D.D., "In Protests, a Nobelist Has an Unfamiliar Role," *New York Times*, 29 January 2011, p. A11.

Kirkpatrick, D.D., "Mubarak Orders Crackdown, With Revolt Sweeping Egypt," *New York Times*, 29 January 2011, p. A1.

Kirkpatrick, D.D., "Egyptians Defiant as Military Does Little to Quash Protests," *New York Times*, 30 January 2011, p. 1.

Kirkpatrick, D.D., "Protest's Old Guard Falls in Behind the Young," *New York Times*, 31 January 2011, p. A1.

Kirkpatrick, D.D., "Mubarak's Grip Is Shaken as Millions Are Called to Protest," *New York Times*, 1 February 2011, p. A1.

Kirkpatrick, D.D., "Google Executive Who Was Jailed Said He Was Part of Online Campaign in Egypt," *New York Times*, 8 February 2011, p. A10.

Kirkpatrick, D.D., "As Egypt Protest Swells, US Sends Specifics Demands," *New York Times*, 9 February 2011, p. A1.

Kirkpatrick, D.D., "Wired, Educated and Shrewd, Young Egyptians Guide Revolt," *New York Times*, 10 February 2011, p. 1.

Kirkpatrick, D.D., "Mubarak Out," *New York Times*, 12 February 2011, p. 1.

Kirkpatrick, D.D. and El-Naggar, M., "Rich, Poor and a Rift Exposed by Unrest," *New York Times*, 31 January 2011, p. A6.

Kirkpatrick, D.D. and Sanger, D.E., "Egypt Officials Seek to Nudge Mubarak Out," *New York Times*, 5 February 2011, p. A1.

Kirkpatrick, D.D. and Sanger, D.E., "After First Talks, Egypt Opposition Vows New Protest," *New York Times*, 7 February 2011, p. A1.

Kirkpatrick, D.D. and Sanger, D.E., "A Tunisian-Egyptian Link That Shook Arab History," *New York Times*, 14 February 2011, p. A1.

Kirkpatrick, D.D. and Slackman, M., "In New Role, Egypt Youths Drive Revolt," *New York Times*, 27 January 2011, p. A1.

Kristoff, N.D., "Exhilarated by the Hope in Cairo," *New York Times*, 1 February 2011, p. A27.

Kristoff, N.D., "Militants, Women and Tahrir Square," *New York Times*, 6 February 2011, "Week in Review," p. 8.

Kulish, N. and Mekhennet, S. "In Alexandria, Protesters Win After a Day of Fierce Fighting with Riot Police," *New York Times*, 29 January 2011, p. A12.

Landler, M., "Obama Cautions Embattled Egyptian Ally Against Violent Repression," *New York Times*, 29 January 2011, p. A1.

Landler, M., "Clinton Calls for 'Orderly Transition' to Greater Freedom in Egypt," *New York Times*, 31 January 2011, p. A6.

Landler, M. and Lehren, A., "State's Secrets; Cables Show US Tack on Egypt: Public Support, Private Pressure," *New York Times*, 28 January 2011, p. A1.

Levinson, C. and Dagher, S., "Rallies Fan Out as Regime Closes Ranks," *Wall Street Journal* (online), 9 February 2011, http://online.wsj.com/article/SB10001424052748704858404576133630107794342.html [accessed 20 June 2011].

Levinson, C., Coker, M., and Bradley, M., "Chaos, Looting Spread as Mubarak Names Key Deputies," *Wall Street Journal* (online), 29 January 2011, http://online.wsj.com/article/SB100014240527487046 53204576111443650347716.html [accessed 20 June 2011].

Lynch, M., "Beyond the Arab Street: Iraq and the Arab Public Sphere," *Politics and Society* 31: 1 (2003), pp. 55–91.

Lynch, M., Glasser, S.B., and Hounshell, B. (eds), *Revolution in the Arab World*, Washington, DC: Foreign Policy, 2011.

Machiavelli, N., *The Discourses* in *The Essential Writings of Niccolo Machiavelli*, translated and edited by Peter Constantine, New York, NY: Modern Library, 2007 [1531].

Mahfouz, N., *Before the Throne: Dialogues with Egypt's Great from Menes to Anwar Sadat*, Cairo: The American University in Cairo Press, 2009 [1983].

Mason, P., "Twenty Reasons Why It's Kicking Off Everywhere," 'Idle Scrawl Blog', BBC (online), 5 February 2011, http://www.bbc.co.uk/blogs/newsnight/paulmason/2011/02/twenty_reasons_why_its_kicking.html [accessed 10 June 2011].

May, C., "Protesters Stand Fast in Cairo's Tahrir Square," *USA Today*, 8 February 2011, p. 4A.

MacFarquhar, N., "Egypt's Respected Military Is Seen as Pivotal in What Happens Next," *New York Times*, 29 January 2011, p. A13.

McGreal, C., "Front: Egypt in Crisis: 'Mubarak is still here, but there's been a revolution in our minds'," *Guardian*, 6 February 2011, p. 4.

Mekhennet, S. and Kulish, N., "With Muslim Brotherhood Set to Join Egypt Protests, Religion's Role May Grow," *New York Times*, 28 January 2011, p. A10.

Michaels, J., "Tech-savvy Youths Led the Way in Egypt Protests; And They Want Seat at the Table in Negotiations," *USA Today*, 7 February 2011, p. 2A.

Miles, H., "The Al Jazeera Effect," in M. Lynch, S.B. Glasser, and B. Hounshell (eds), *Revolution in the Arab World*, Washington, DC: Foreign Policy, 2011.

Miller, T., "In the Mideast, Days of Tumult," *New York Times*, 29 January 2011, p. A22.

Mohamed, Z., Hazou, V., Degner, D., al-Atraqchi, F., and Mayton, J., "The Word on the Street: The Protests This Week in Egypt Against the Mubarak Regime Have Gripped the Country," *Guardian*, 28 January 2011, "G2", p. 6.

*Le Monde*, "Editorial; Il Faut Appeler un Dictateur un Dictateur," *Le Monde*, 2 February 2011, p. 1.

*Le Monde*, "Le Régime Moubarak Contre-attaque," *Le Monde*, 4 February 2011, p. 1.

*Le Monde*, "Repères; Chronologie," *Le Monde*, 5 February 2011, p. 19.

Montefiore, S.S., "Every Revolution Is Revolutionary in Its Own Way," *New York Times*, 27 March 2011, "Review", p. 11.

Mubarak, H., "I will not … accept to hear foreign dictations," *Washington Post* (online), 10 February 2011, http://www.washingtonpost.com/wp-dyn/content/article/2011/02/10/AR2011021005290.html [accessed 10 June 2011].

*New York Times*, "Beyond Mubarak," *New York Times*, 2 February 2011, p. A22.

*New York Times*, "From Sadat to Mubarak: A Reminiscence, and a Prayer," *New York Times*, 3 February 2011, http://www.nytimes.com/2011/02/03/opinion/lweb03cairo.html [accessed 12 June 2011].

*New York Times*, "Letters," *New York Times*, 4 February 2011, p. A12.

*New York Times*, "Mr. Suleiman's Empty Promises. Editorial," *New York Times*, 9 February 2011, p. A26.

*New York Times*, "Egypt's Moment," *New York Times*, 12 February 2011, p. A20.

Nixon, R., "US Groups Helped Nurture Arab Opposition," *New York Times*, 15 April 2011, p. A1.

Osman, T., *Egypt on the Brink: From Nasser to Mubarak*, New Haven, CT: Yale University Press, 2010.

Pollack, K., "Could al Qaeda Hijack Egypt's Revolution?" *Wall Street Journal* (online), 9 February 2011, http://online.wsj.com/article/SB10 001424052748704843304576126393150812416.html [accessed 20 June 2011].

Prail, B., "In the Mideast, Days of Tumult, 'To the Editor'." *New York Times*, 29 January 2011, p. A22.

Preston, J., "While Facebook Plays a Star Role in the Revolts, Its Executives Stay Offstage," *New York Times*, 15 February 2011, p. 10.

Rampoldi, G., "La Rivolta che Cambia la Storia Araba," *La Repubblica*, 29 January 2011, http://www.repubblica.it/esteri/2011/01/29/news/ la_rivolta_che_cambia_la_storia_araba-11796023 [accessed 22 April 2011].

*La Repubblica*, "Scontri e Morti in Tutto l'Egitto. Il Presidente in TV: 'E' Complotto," *La Repubblica*, 29 January 2011, http://www.repubblica. it/esteri/2011/01/29/news/scontri_e_morti_in_tutto_l_egitto_il_ presidente_in_tv_e_complotto-11795852 [accessed 22 April 2011].

*La Repubblica*, "'Mubarak Vattene. Basta Dittatura,' La Protesta degli Egiziani a Roma," *La Repubblica*, 31 January 2011, http://roma. repubblica.it/cronaca/2011/01/31/news/mubarak_vattene_basta_ dittatura_la_protesta_degli_egiziani_a_roma-11893136 [accessed 15 April 2011].

*La Repubblica*, "Manifestanti Ancora in Piazza al Cairo Usa Premono per Cambiamento," *La Repubblica*, 5 February 2011, http://www. repubblica.it/esteri/2011/02/05/news/sostituiti_vertici_partito_ mubarak_lascia-12100571 [accessed 22 April 2011].

Rauer, V., "Symbols in Action: Willy Brandt's Kneefall at the Warsaw Memorial," in J.C. Alexander, B. Giesen, and J. Mason (eds), *Social Performance: Symbolic Action, Cultural Pragmatics, and Ritual*, New York, NY: Cambridge University Press, 2006, pp. 257–82.

Ringmar, E., "The Power of Metaphor: Consent, Dissent & Revolution," in R. Mole (ed.) *Discursive Constructions of Identity in European Politics*, London: Palgrave Macmillan, 2007.

Ringmar, E., "Performing International Relations: Two East Asian Alternatives to the Westphalian Order," *International Organization* 66 (2012): p. 2.

Rodrigues, J., "Egypt: Timeline," *Guardian*, 11 February 2011, p. 4.

Rosenberg, T., "Revolution U," in M. Lynch, S.B. Glasser, and B. Hounshell (eds), *Revolution in the Arab World*, Washington, DC: Foreign Policy, 2011.

Sadiki, L., *The Search for Arab Democracy*, New York, NY: Columbia University Press, 2004.

Said, A., "Uprising in Egypt: America in the Egyptian Revolution," The Immanent Frame [blog], 4 April 2011, http://blogs.ssrc.org/tif/2011/04/11/america-in-the-egyptian-revolution [accessed 15 June 2011]

Said, A., "On the Communication During the Internet Blackout in Egypt and Generally During the 18 Days of the Egyptian Revolution," Ethnographic Field Notes, unpublished manuscript, 22 April 2011.

Said, E., *Orientalism*, New York, NY: Vintage, 1979.

Sanger, D.E., "As Mubarak Digs In, Complications for US Policy," *New York Times*, 6 February 2011, p. A12.

Sanger, D.E., "When Armies Decide," *New York Times*, 20 February 2011, "Week in Review," p. 1.

Scuto, F., "El Baradei, l'Uomo del Destino 'Oggi Nasce un Paese Nuovo'," *La Repubblica*, 1 February 2011, http://www.repubblica.it/esteri/2011/02/01/news/baradei_uomo_destino-11904735 [accessed 15 April 2011].

Seib, G., "Now Dawning: The Next Era of Middle East History," *Wall Street Journal* (online), 31 January 2011, http://online.wsj.com/article/SB10001424052748704254304576116110110596324.html [accessed 20 June 2011].

Shadid, A., "Seizing Control of Their Lives and Wondering What's Next," *New York Times*, 30 January 2011, p. A1.

Shadid, A., "Yearning for Respect, Arabs Find a Voice," *New York Times*, 30 January 2011, p. A10.

Shadid, A., "In the Euphoria of the Crowd, No Party or Leader Unifies the Opposition," *New York Times*, 1 February 2011, p. A11.

Shadid, A., "Mubarak Won't Run Again, But Stays; Obama urges a Faster Shift of Power," *New York Times*, 2 February 2011, p. A1.

Shadid, A., "Street Battle Over the Arab Future," *New York Times*, 3 February 2011, p. 1.

Shadid, A., "Egypt Officials Widen Crackdown; US in Talks for Mubarak to Quit," *New York Times*, 4 February 2011, p. A1.

Shadid, A., "Discontented Within Egypt Face Power of Old Elites," *New York Times*, 5 February 2011, p. A7.

Shadid, A., "At Night in Tahrir Square, Cairo Protest Gives Way to Poetry and Performances," *New York Times*, 7 February 2011, p. A9.

Shadid, A., "Egypt's Leaders Seek to Project Air of Normalcy," *New York Times*, 8 February 2011, p. A1.

Shadid, A., "After Tahrir, Uncharted Ground," *New York Times*, 12 February 2011, p. A1.

Shadid, A. and Kirkpatrick, D.D., "In Egypt, Opposition Unifies Around Government Critic," *New York Times*, 31 January 2011, p. 1.

Shadid, A. and Kirkpatrick, D.D., "Mubarak Won't Quit, Stoking Revolt's Fury and Resolve," *New York Times*, 11 February 2011, p. A1.

Shadid, A. and Kirkpatrick, D.D., "After Tahrir, Unchartered Ground," *New York Times*, 12 February 2011, p. A1.

Shenker, J., "Egypt Awaits Nationwide 'Day of Revolution'," *Guardian*, 25 January 2011, p. 22.

Shenker, J., "Mubarak Regime in Crisis as Biggest Anti-government Demonstrations in a Generation Sweep across Egypt," *Guardian*, 26 January 2011.

Shenker, J., "Revolt Spreads to Egypt: Violent Clashes on Streets of Cairo," *Guardian*, 26 January 2011, p. 1.

Shenker, J., "Teargas and Baton Charges Sweep Protesters Off Cairo's Streets," *Guardian*, 26 January 2011, p. 22.

Shenker, J., "Egypt: Journalist's Detention: Bloody and Bruised in the Back of a Truck, Destination Unknown." *Guardian*, 27 January 2011, p. 18.

Shenker, J. and Black, I., "Egypt: Change is Coming, Says ElBaradei as US Calls for 'orderly transition'," *Guardian*, 31 January 2011, p. 1.

Shenker, J. and Khalili, M., "Day of No Departure: Cairo's Biggest Turnout Yet, but Mubarak Clings On," *Guardian*, 5 February 2011, p. 1.

Shenker, J., Beaumont, P., Black, I., and McGreal, C., "Egypt: Power to the People: Mubarak Finally Bows to the Inevitable," *Guardian*, 2 February 2011, p. 1.

Sherwood, H., Chrisafis, A., Chulov, M., and Balousha, H., "Fall of Mubarak: Hope and Fear. How the Arab World Reacted," *Guardian*, 12 February 2011, p. 4.

Slackman, M., "In Mideast Activism, a New Tilt Away from Ideology," *New York Times*, 23 January 2011, p. 10.

Slackman, M., "Compact Between Egypt and Its Leader Erodes," *New York Times*, 29 January 2011, p. 11.

Slackman, M., "Omar Suleiman: A Choice Likely to Please the Military, not the Crowds," *New York Times*, 30 January 2011, p. A10.

Slackman, M., "A Brittle Leader, Appearing Strong," *New York Times*, 12 February 2011, p. A1.

Soueif, A., "Fittingly, It's the Young of the Country Who Are Leading Us," *Guardian*, 28 January 2011, p. 1.

Soueif, A., "Egypt: 'For Everyone Here, There's No Turning Back'," *Guardian*, 2 February 2011, p. 1.

Soueif, A., "Fall of Mubarak: 'Look at the streets of Egypt ... this is what hope looks like'," *Guardian*, 12 February 2011, p. 2.

Soueif, A., "Protesters Reclaim the Spirit of Egypt," BBC News, 13 February 2011, http://www.bbc.co.uk/news/world-middle-east-12393795 [accessed 22 April 2011].

Springborg, P., "Politics, Primordialism, and Orientalism: Marx, Aristotle, and the Myth of the Gemenschaft," *American Political Science Review* 80: 1 (1986), pp. 185-211.

Springborg, P., *Western Republicanism and the Oriental Prince*, London: Polity, 1992.

Stanley, A., "As Crisis Plays Out Live on TV, Commentators Hurl Brickbats at One Another," *New York Times*, 5 February 2011, p. A7.

Stelter, B., "From Afar, News about Egypt," *New York Times*, 14 February 2011, p. B4.

Tait, R., "Front: Egypt: 28 Hours in the Dark Heart of Egypt's Torture Machine," *Guardian*, 10 February 2011, p. 4.

Tisdall, S., "World Briefing: New Wave of Protest Takes Mubarak Out of Comfort Zone," *Guardian*, 26 January 2011, p. 22.

Todd, E., *Le Rendez-vous des Civilization*, Paris: Seuil, 2007.

Todd, E., "Interview by Lara Ricci," *Il Sole 24 Ore* (online), 26 February 2011, http://lararicci.blog.ilsole24ore.com [accessed 12 June 2011].

Turner, V., *The Ritual Process*, Chicago, IL: Aldine, 1969.

*USA Today*, "Rumblings abroad test American ideals," *USA Today*, 27 January 2011, p. 8A.

*USA Today*, "Anti-Mubarak Protest Brings Moment of Truth for US," *USA Today*, 31 January 2011, p. 8A.

Valli, B., "Egitto, Nella Piazza che Grida 'Da qui non ce ne andiamo'," *La Repubblica*, 5 February 2011, http://www.repubblica.it/ esteri/2011/02/05/news/egitto_nella_piazza_che_grida_da_qui_ non_ce_ne_andiamo-12081033 [accessed 22 April 2011].

Valli, B., "La Beffa Finale del Faraone di Plastica," *La Repubblica*, 11 February 2011, http://www.repubblica.it/esteri/2011/02/11/news/ beffa_faraone-12321773 [accessed 22 April 2011].

*Wall Street Journal*, "Celebrations Follow Resignation in Egypt," *Wall Street Journal* (online), 12 February 2011, http://blogs.wsj.com/ photojournal/2011/02/11/celebrations-follow-resignation-in-egypt/ [accessed 20 June 2011].

Walzer, M., *The Revolution of the Saints*, Cambridge, MA: Harvard University Press, 1965.

"We Are All Khaled Said," Facebook, 26, 27, 28 January 2011, https://www. facebook.com/#!/elshaheeed.co.uk [accessed 13 March 2011].

Worth, R., "Extreme Measures: How a Single Match Can Ignite a Revolution," *New York Times*, 23 January 2011, "Week in Review", p. 4.

Worth, R., "On Al Jazeera, a Revolution Televised Despite Hurdles," *New York Times*, 29 January 2011, p. A11.

Yaffa, J., "Downloading the Uprising; Can Technology's Tools Liberate Those Living Under Political Repression?", *Wall Street Journal* (online), 4 February 2011, http://online.wsj.com/article/SB1000142 405274870415010457612275178502 9870.html [accessed 20 June 2011].

Youssef, M., "Quotation of the Day," *New York Times*, 27 January 2011, p. A2.

Zimmer, B., "How the War of Words Was Won," *New York Times*, 13 February 2011, "Week in Review," p. 4.

Zizek, S., "Comment: What We Are Witnessing Is the Miracle of Tahrir Square," *Guardian*, 11 February 2011, p. 38.

# Index